Winter Wonders

15 Quilts & Projects to Celebrate the Season

Edited by Jennifer Rounds
& Catherine Comyns

C&T PUBLISHING

© 2004 Nihon Vogue Co., Ltd

All text, illustrations and photographs selected from "Quilts Japan"
Originally published by Nihon Vogue Co., Ltd.
Copyright (c) 1997, 1998, 2000, 2001 by Nihon Vogue Co., Ltd.
All rights reserved
English translation rights arranged with Nihon Vogue Co., Ltd.,
through Japan Foreign-Rights Centre.
Publisher: Amy Marson
Editorial Director: Gailen Runge
Developmental Editor: Jennifer Rounds
Technical Editors: Catherine Comyns, Sharon Page Ritchie
Proofreader: Stacy Chamness
Design Director: Diane Pedersen
Cover Designer: Kristy A. Konitzer
Book Designer: John Cram
Illustrator: Richard Sheppard
Production Assistant: Kirstie L. McCormick
Photography: Norio Ando, Akinori Miyashita, Masaki Yamamoto,
Published by C&T Publishing, Inc., P.O. Box 1456, Lafayette, California, 94549
Front cover: *Christmas Boxes* Quilt (Page 38) by Yoshie Ishiguro, Photo by Norio Ando
Back cover: Detail of *Dancing Santas Quilt* (Page 30) by Mayumi Hattori, Photo by Akinori Miyashita,
Christmas Cats (Page 17) by Kazumi Imai, Photo by Norio Ando, *Angel Ornaments* (Page 35) by Chieko
Ishizaki, Photo by Norio Ando

Attention Copy Shops: Please note the following exception—Publisher gives permission to photocopy
pages 9-16, 19, 24, 26, 28-29, 34, 37, 44, 46, 49, 55, 60 and 62 for personal use only.

Attention Teachers: C&T Publishing, Inc. encourages you to use this book as a text for teaching.

Contact us at 800-284-1114 or www.ctpub.com for more information about the C&T Teachers Program.

We take great care to ensure that the information included in this book is accurate and presented in good
faith, but no warranty is provided nor results guaranteed. Having no control over the choices of materials or
procedures used, neither the author nor C&T Publishing, Inc. shall have any liability to any person or entity
with respect to any loss or damage caused directly or indirectly by the information contained in this book.
For your convenience, we post an up-to-date listing of corrections on our web page (www.ctpub.com). If a
correction is not already noted, please contact our customer service department at ctinfo@ctpub.com or at
P.O. Box 1456, Lafayette, California, 94549.

Trademarked (™) and Registered Trademark (®) names are used throughout this book. Rather than use the
symbols with every occurrence of a trademark and registered trademark name, we are using the names only
in the editorial fashion and to the benefit of the owner, with no intention of infringement.

Library of Congress Cataloging-in-Publication Data

Winter wonders : 15 quilts & projects to celebrate the season / edited
by Jennifer Rounds and Catherine Comyns.
     p. cm.
Includes index.
  ISBN 1-57120-231-5 (paper trade)
  1. Patchwork--Patterns. 2. Quilting. 3. Appliqué--Patterns. 4.
Christmas decorations. 5. Quilts--Japan. I. Rounds, Jennifer.
II. Comyns, Catherine.
  TT835.W553 2004
  746.46'041--dc22
                              2003020030

Printed in China
10 9 8 7 6 5 4 3 2 1

Table of Contents

Angel Garland (See page 35 for instructions)

Introduction

It's amazing how the traditions of an essentially Western Christian winter holiday have traveled across the globe. People in the remotest places know about Santa Claus, Christmas trees, and present-stuffed stockings. Nowhere is this more true than in Japan. The symbols, stories, and rituals of Christmas have been adopted by the Japanese people and interpreted in marvelous and surprising ways.

Winter Wonders: 15 Quilts & Projects to Celebrate the Season spotlights the inventive genius of Japanese quiltmakers who've created a collection of traditional winter quilts with familiar Christmas themes, color palettes, and symbols that is both unexpected and delightful. By giving us another view of our traditions, their quilts and projects refresh our perspective and invigorate our craft.

Why would a culture that has such different religious beliefs create an abundance of Christmas-themed projects? In part, the Japanese people have been fascinated and profoundly influenced by Western exports of popular culture and literature. Classic movies like *White Christmas,* starring Bing Crosby, and *It's a Wonderful Life,* starring Jimmy Stewart, have traveled across the world and introduced legions of people to our winter holiday. Add stories about kinder, gentler times like *Anne of Green Gables*, a perpetual favorite among Japanese readers, and the Christmas season becomes a somewhat mythic and magical place where peace reigns and dreams come true—a snow-covered town filled with holiday cheer.

The 15 projects in *Winter Wonders* will take you to that very special place:

 Gingerbread Wreaths Quilt: An enchanting larger-scale quilt decorated with tasty wreaths of gingerbread cookies.

 Scrappy Holiday Quilt and Bedside Rug: A full-size quilt perfect for dreaming of those fabled dancing sugarplums, and a tiny bedside rug to protect little toes from the chill of a winter morning.

Dancing Santas Quilt: A jazzy wall hanging with a dozen Santas cartwheeling across its surface.

 Christmas Boxes Quilt: A remarkable full-size quilt with unusual coloration and embellishments and featuring an innovative spin on a traditional Tumbling Blocks pattern.

 Star-lit Christmas Tree Quilt: A dazzling quilt that blends piecing and appliqué to create a sparkling, snow-filled winter scene.

 Silver Trees Quilt & Pillow: A perfect full-size winter quilt and napping pillow that capture the silvery quiet of a wintry forest.

 Little projects perfect for holiday giving: *Angel Ornament and Garland, Braided Christmas Wreath, Christmas Cats, Pinecone Party Favor, Reindeer Redwork Pillow, Winter Scene Appliqué Pillow.*

Like our first two titles, *A Bouquet of Quilts* and *A Floral Affair* —which also feature projects from Nihon Vogue's *Quilts Japan,* this book continues the tradition of providing both American standard and metric measurements for the projects. In *Winter Wonders,* we've raised the bar and included some heirloom projects to challenge quiltmakers. Techniques still range from simple piecing to appliqué, but this time we include paper piecing, Y-seaming, and embellishing. Note that in some instances we have simplified the projects for construction ease.

As always, we thank the wonderful quiltmakers from Japan whose creativity and dedication to our craft never cease to amaze us. We are honored to present your work to a broader audience.

Gingerbread Wreaths Quilt

Gingerbread Wreaths Quilt

MADE BY: Misuzu Okuzumi
PHOTO BY: Akinori Miyashita

FINISHED SIZE: 83½" × 83½" (209 cm × 209 cm)
FINISHED BLOCK SIZE: 15" × 15" (37.5 cm × 37.5 cm)
TECHNIQUES: Paper piecing/Appliqué/Embroidery

Imagine a storybook holiday town where each house glows with lights and décor and the enticing scents of gingerbread waft on the air beckoning weary shoppers to their hearths for warm drinks and delicious treats. Add your own touches to the tasty cookies or, if your tastes run to traditional gingerbread fare, ice them with white fabric paint to re-create the classic gingerbread motif.

FABRIC REQUIREMENTS

U.S.		METRIC
6½ yards	White for appliquéd and pieced blocks, binding, and sashing	5.3 meters
1⅜ yards	Green for sashing and inner border	1.2 meters
¾ yard	Honey and golden brown tones for gingerbread cookies and tree tunks	70 cm
⅝ yard, total	Assorted plaids for wreath bows	60 cm, total
4 yards, total	Assorted print scraps for gingerbread cookies, heart posts, pieced borders	3.6 meters, total
½ yard	Dark green for trees	50 cm
7⅜ yards	Backing	6.6 meters
88" × 88"	Batting	220 cm × 220 cm
	Embroidery floss for faces and hair	

CUTTING

U.S.	WHITE	METRIC
16½" × 16½"	Appliquéd blocks: Cut 16.	42 cm × 42 cm
Note: These blocks are cut slightly larger than necessary and will be trimmed after completing the appliqué.		
3½" × 3½"	Posts: Cut 9.	9 cm × 9 cm
Note: These blocks are cut slightly larger than necessary and will be trimmed after completing the appliqué.		
1¼" × 7"	House sashing: Cut 40.	3.2 cm × 17.8 cm
2¼" × 350"	Binding: Cut on the straight of grain and double folded.	5.7 cm × 870 cm

U.S.	GREEN	METRIC
2½" × 15"	Sashing: Cut 24.	6.4 cm × 39.4 cm
2½" × 66½"	Side inner borders: Cut 2.	6.4 cm × 168.9 cm
2½" × 70½"	Top and bottom inner borders: Cut 2.	6.4 cm × 179.1 cm

Gingerbread Wreath Block Assembly

Note: Each wreath block contains 7 cookies and 1 bow. Make 16 wreath blocks.

1. Use the templates provided and the fabric of your choice to make the gingerbread cookies, plaid bows, and heart posts. Be sure to add a turn-under seam allowance to each piece.

2. Use the appliqué method of your choice to make the gingerbread cookie wreath blocks. Stitch the facial features and hair details with embroidery floss after completing the appliqué. Trim each block to measure 15½" × 15½" (39.4 cm × 39.4 cm).

3. Appliqué 9 heart posts. Trim each heart post to measure 2½" × 2½" (6.4 cm × 6.4 cm).

4. Alternately sew 4 gingerbread cookies wreath blocks to 3 sashing strips. Press the seams toward the sashing strips. Make 4 rows.

5. Alternately sew 3 heart posts to 4 sashing strips. Press the seams toward the sashing strips.

6. Alternately sew the 3 heart post rows between the 4 gingerbread cookies wreath rows. Press the seams toward the post rows.

7. Sew a side inner border to each side of the quilt top. Press the seams toward the borders.

8. Sew the top and bottom inner borders to the quilt top. Press the seams toward the borders.

Paper Piecing Primer

1. Photocopy each unit that will be paper pieced as many times as indicated.

2. Cut out the fabric pieces for each unit slightly larger than necessary—approximately $1/2$" (1.2 cm) or larger on every side.

3. Follow the numbering sequence on each pattern to construct each unit.

4. Pin the first piece of fabric right side up to the appropriate spot on the non-printed side of the paper. Hold the paper up to the light to make sure the piece covers its outlined area completely, including the seam allowance.

5. Place and pin the right side of the fabric swatch cut for the second shape on top of the fabric swatch for first one. Again, check to be sure that both pieces extend a generous $1/4$" (0.6 cm) or more beyond their shared sewing line.

6. With the printed side up, sew along the line. Start a couple of stitches before the sewing line and extend the sewn line a couple of stitches beyond the end. Make sure to use a short stitch length (15 to 20 stitches per inch or 1.5–1.8) and a slightly larger needle (90/14). These precautions ease paper removal and maintain stitch integrity when tearing away the paper.

7. Open the sewn piece and finger press. Hold the pattern up to the light to make sure the fabric swatches cover both shapes completely, including the seam allowance.

8. Fold back the second swatch to the first swatch and trim the shared seam to $1/4$" (0.6 cm) and then finger press the second swatch back in place. Repeat these steps to complete the unit.

9. Press the unit after completing the sewing. Trim a $1/4$" (0.6 cm) seam allowance around the finished unit. Do not remove the paper until all the completed units have been sewn together. Use tweezers to remove paper remnants.

Tree Blocks and House Blocks Assembly

Note: The templates for the house border strips are organized according to house width: Template A houses are 8" (20.3 cm) wide, the Template B house is 7" (17.8 cm) wide, Template C houses are $6 1/2$" (16.5 cm) wide, and the Template D house is 4" (10.2 cm) wide. Each border strip requires 4 Template A Houses, 1 Template B house, 3 Template C houses, and 1 Template D house. Choose the most pleasing assortment.

1. Paper piece the tree blocks and the house blocks in the order indicated by the numbers. Make 4 tree blocks and 36 house blocks. Press each block.

2. Select the blocks for a border and sew a white sashing strip between each house and at either end of the border strip. Press the seams toward the sashing strips. Make 4 rows of houses for the outer borders.

Borders

1. Sew a row of houses to opposite sides of the quilt top. Press the seams toward the side inner borders.

2. Sew a tree to each end of the 2 remaining house border rows. Press the seams toward the white border strips.

3. Sew the remaining borders to the top and bottom of the quilt. Press the seams toward the top and bottom inner borders.

Finishing

1. Layer and baste the quilt top with the batting and backing.

2. Quilt a diagonal grid in each gingerbread cookie wreath block. Quilt hearts in the sashing and inner borders. Quilt straight lines perpendicular to the edge of the quilt in the outer pieced borders.

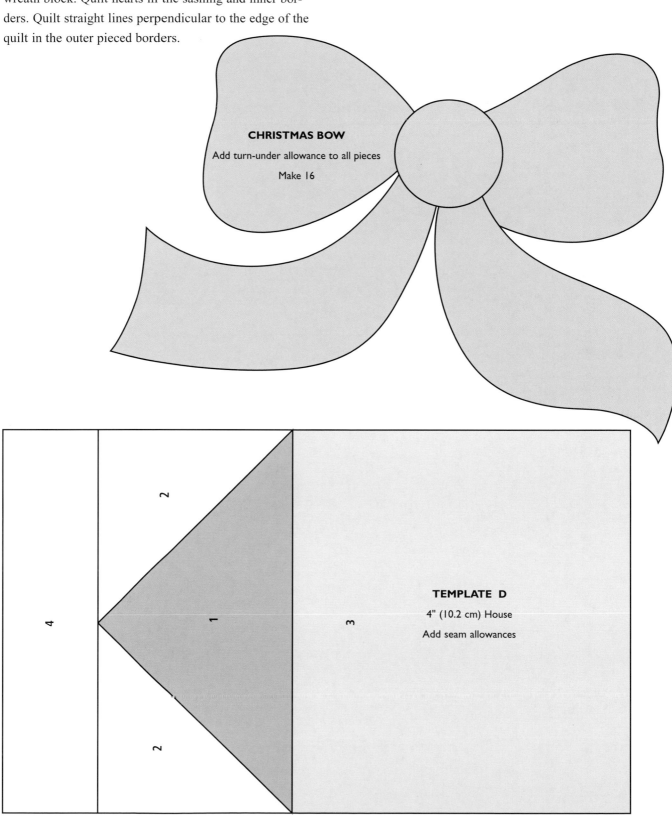

CHRISTMAS BOW

Add turn-under allowance to all pieces

Make 16

TEMPLATE D

4" (10.2 cm) House

Add seam allowances

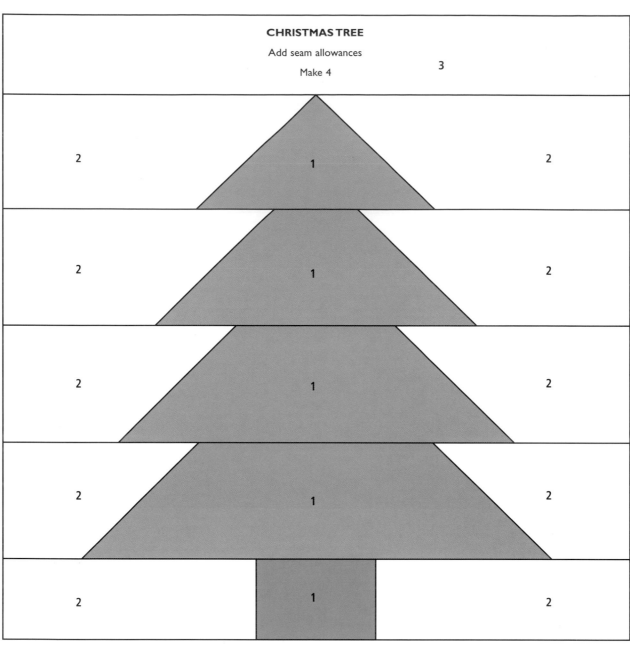

CHRISTMAS TREE

Add seam allowances

Make 4

3

2   1   2

2   1   2

2   1   2

2   1   2

2   1   2

GINGERBREAD GIRL

Add turn-under
allowance to all pieces

Make 56

TEMPLATE B

7" (17.8 cm) House

6

Add seam allowances

| 3 | 2 | 1 | 2 | 3 |

5

3

5

| 4 | 2 | | 2 | 4 |

1

| 4 | 3 | 4 |

| 2 | 1 | 2 | 1 | 2 | 1 | 2 |

3

3

3

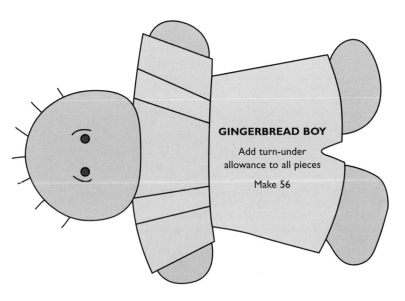

GINGERBREAD BOY

Add turn-under
allowance to all pieces

Make 56

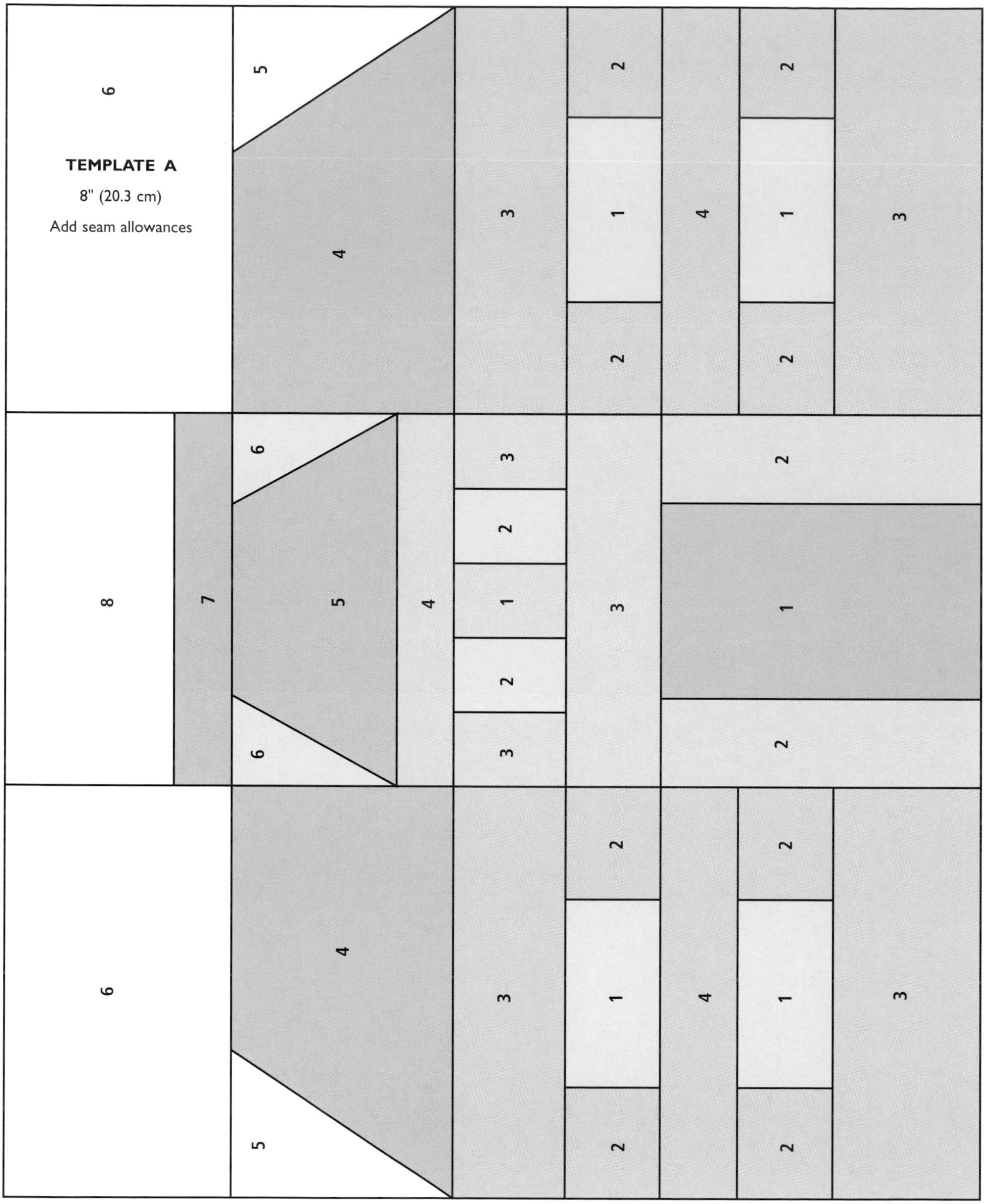

TEMPLATE A

8" (20.3 cm)

Add seam allowances

6

5

4

3

2

1

2

4

2

1

2

3

8

7

6

5

4

3

2

1

2

3

3

2

1

2

6

6

4

3

2

1

2

4

2

1

2

3

5

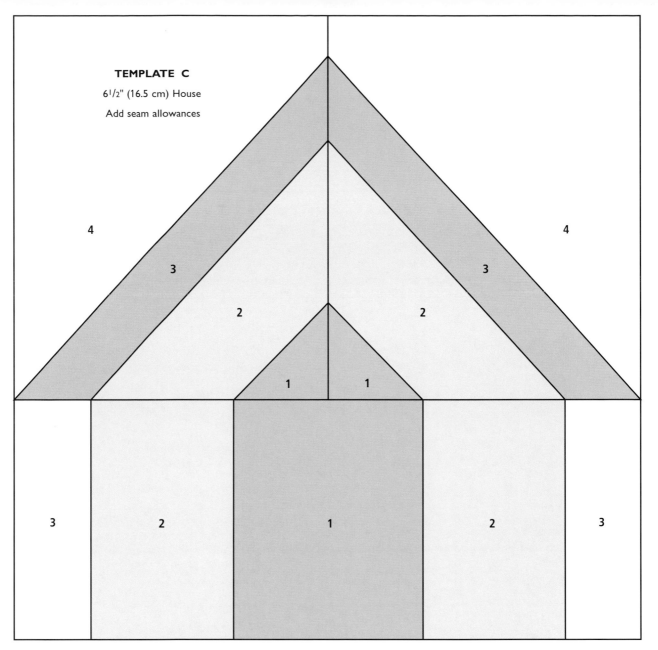

TEMPLATE C

6¹/₂" (16.5 cm) House

Add seam allowances

TEMPLATE A

8" (20.3 cm) wide

Enlarge 150%

Add seam allowances

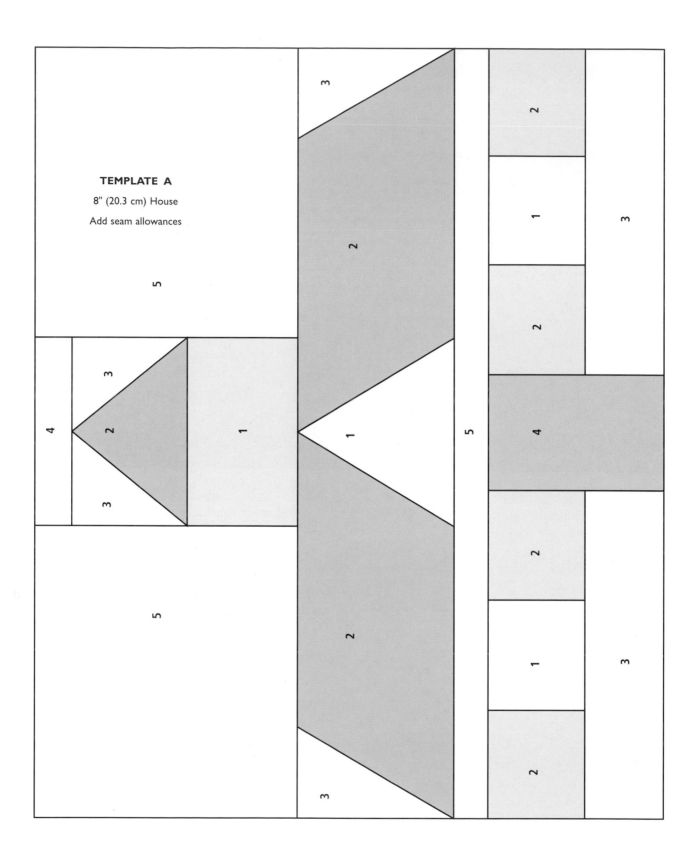

TEMPLATE A

8" (20.3 cm) House

Add seam allowances

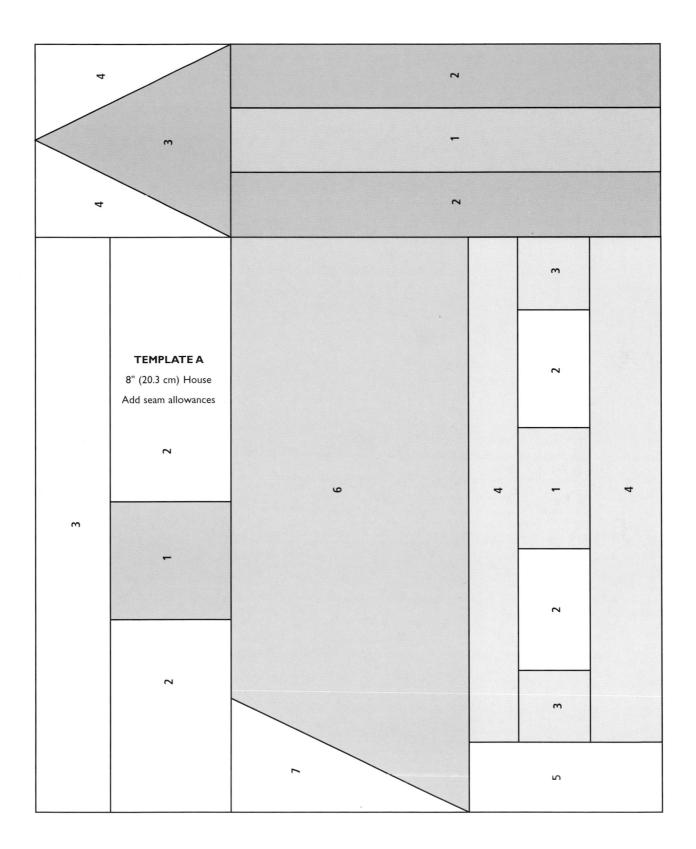

TEMPLATE A

8" (20.3 cm) House

Add seam allowances

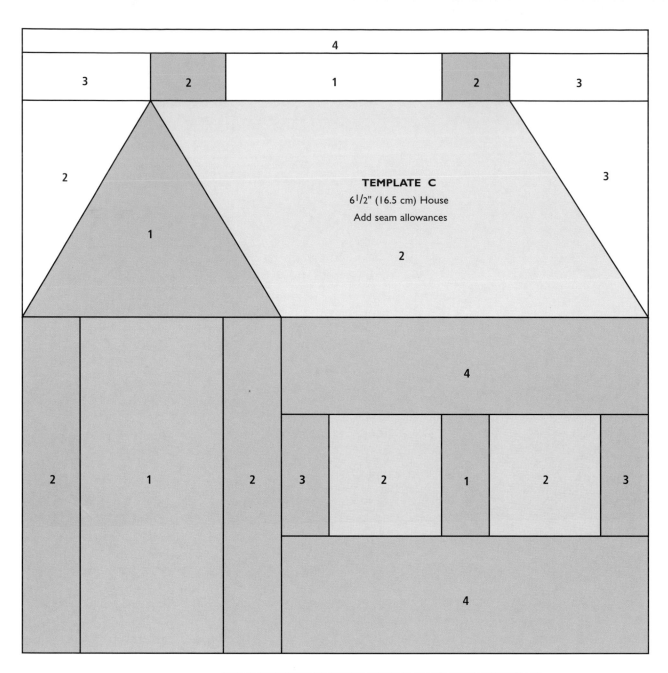

TEMPLATE C
6 1/2" (16.5 cm) House
Add seam allowances

TEMPLATE C
6 1/2" (16.5 cm) House
Add seam allowances
Enlarge 150%

HEART FOR POSTS

Add turn-under allowance

Make 9

Christmas Cats

MADE BY: Kazumi Imai
PHOTO BY: Norio Ando
FINISHED SIZE: 10³/4" × 12¹/2" (27 cm × 31 cm)
TECHNIQUES: Piecing/Embroidery

Invite Mr. and Mrs. Christmas Cat to your holiday festivities. They're dressed in stars and ready to shine. For easier and faster piecing, use scraps from an old quilt or orphan blocks to add the decorative element to the cats' bodies. We've included Le Moyne Star instructions just in case you'd like to make the cats as shown.

PROJECT REQUIREMENTS

U.S.		METRIC
12" x 14" or	Section of scrap quilt, orphan blocks, or	30 cm x 35 cm or
¹/4 yard, total	assorted scraps for pillow front and pieced stars	10 cm, total
³/8 yard	Muslin for lining	30 cm
³/8 yard	Backing	30 cm
1 skein	Embroidery floss for eyes and paws	1 skein
12 oz	Fiberfill	340 grams
¹/2 yard	Ribbon for bow tie	45 cm

CUTTING

U.S.	PILLOW FRONT	METRIC
12" x 14"	Pieced scraps with Le Moyne Stars or 1 piece cut to size.	30 cm x 35 cm

U.S.	LE MOYNE STARS	METRIC
	Note: The following cutting directions will make 1 star.	
Template A	Star points: Cut 4 from 2 different fabrics or 8 from 1 fabric.	Template A
Template B	Star sides: Cut 4.	Template B
Template C	Star corners: Cut 4.	Template C

U.S.	MUSLIN	METRIC
12" x 14"	Lining: Cut 1.	30 cm x 35 cm

U.S.	BACKING	METRIC
12" x 14"	Piece scraps to measurement, or cut 1 piece to this size.	30 cm x 35 cm

Le Moyne Star Assembly

1. Cut 4 diamonds each from 2 different fabrics or 8 diamonds from 1 fabric.

2. Sew 1 diamond to 1 side of a side triangle. Start sewing $^1/_4$" (0.6 cm) away from the inner points. Backstitch and complete the seam. Finger-press the seam toward the diamond.

3. Repeat for the second diamond of this pair and sew to the other side of the triangle. Finger press the seam toward the diamond.

4. Repeat with the 3 remaining diamond pairs.

5. Sew a corner square between 2 diamond units. Start sewing $^1/_4$" (0.6 cm) away from the inner corner. Backstitch and complete the seam. Make 2 half-star units.

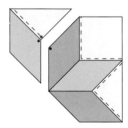

Sewing a half-star unit

6. Press the seam between the diamonds open. Press the corner squares toward the diamonds.

7. Sew 2 corner squares to 1 of the half-star units, taking care not to sew into the inner corner.

8. Sew the half-star units together at the corner squares. Complete the stars by sewing the remaining seam between the star points. Press.

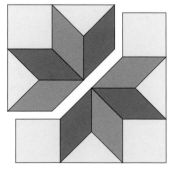

Constructing a Le Moyne star block

Project Assembly

1. Assemble randomly cut fabric and pieced blocks to measure 12" x 14" (30 cm x 35 cm) or use 1 fabric piece cut to size.

2. Layer and baste the pillow front with batting and lining. Quilt random lines and circles as desired.

3. Trace the enlarged cat pattern onto the pieced front. Transfer cat features and embroider before cutting out the cat. Use 2 strands of embroidery floss and a stem stitch to embroider the eyes and paws on the indicated lines.

4. Stay-stitch $^1/_8$" (0.3 cm) inside of the drawn line. Cut on the drawn line. Trace and cut another cat shape from the backing fabric.

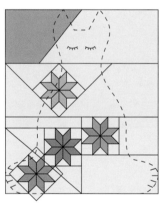
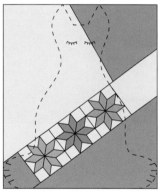

5. Pin the pillow front and back right sides together. Use a $^1/_4$" (0.6 cm) seam allowance to sew the pieces together, leaving an opening at the bottom.

6. Turn the cat pillow cover right side out. Stuff firmly with fiberfill. Close the opening with hand stitches. Add a ribbon bow tie to the boy cat.

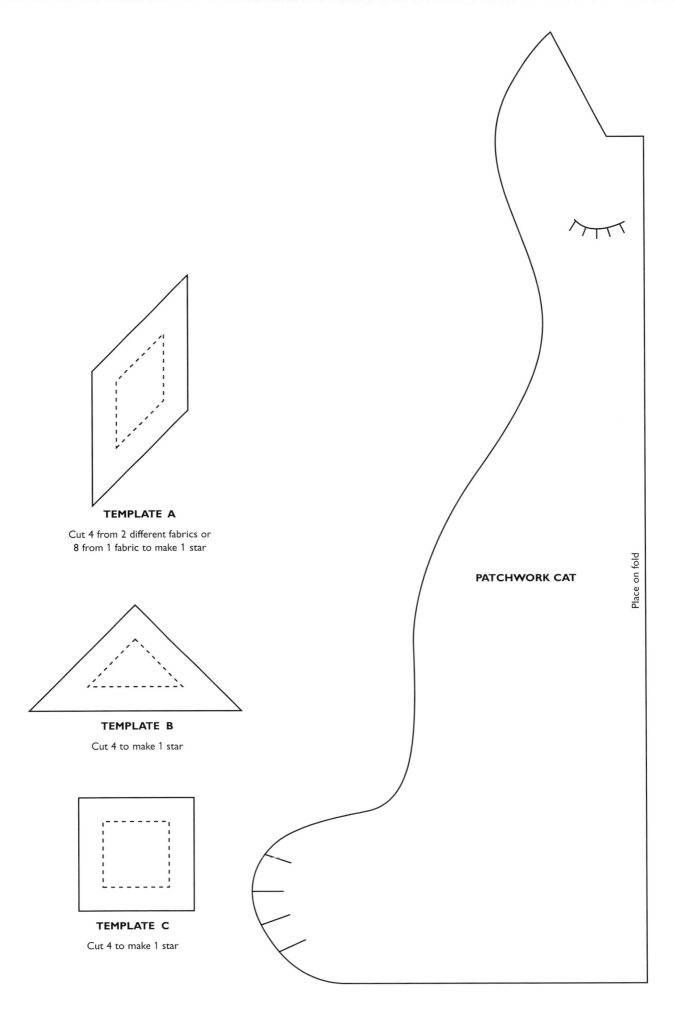

TEMPLATE A

Cut 4 from 2 different fabrics or
8 from 1 fabric to make 1 star

TEMPLATE B

Cut 4 to make 1 star

TEMPLATE C

Cut 4 to make 1 star

PATCHWORK CAT

Place on fold

Scrappy Holiday Projects

Scrappy Holiday Quilt
MADE BY: Reiko Washizawa
PHOTO BY: Akinori Miyashita

FINISHED SIZE: 80 1/2" × 104 1/2" (201.3 cm × 261.3 cm)
FINISHED BLOCK SIZE: 8" × 8" (20 cm × 20 cm)
TECHNIQUES: Piecing

Here's your opportunity to run wild through stashes and stashes of Christmas-themed fabric. This bed–size quilt from a renowned Japanese quilting instructor has a wonderful scrappy feel and a strong visual impact with its yellow and green accents, while large-scale print blocks add visual relief. This project can be easily adapted for strip piecing.

FABRIC REQUIREMENTS

U.S.		METRIC
2 1/2 yards, total	Assorted large-scale prints	2 meters, total
2 1/8 yards, total	Assorted medium-scale prints	1.8 meters, total
3 3/8 yards, total	Assorted small-scale prints	3.1 meters, total
7/8 yard	Yellow print	70 cm
1 3/4 yard	Green print for pieced blocks and binding	1.6 meters
6 yards	Backing	5.4 meters
84" × 108"	Batting	2.1 meters × 2.7 meters
1/4" diameter	Red buttons: 312	0.6 cm diameter

CUTTING

U.S.	ASSORTED LARGE-SCALE PRINTS	METRIC
8 1/2" × 8 1/2"	Squares: Cut 34.	21.2 cm × 21.2 cm

U.S.	ASSORTED MEDIUM-SCALE PRINTS	METRIC
4 1/2" × 8 1/2"	Rectangles: Cut 22.	11.2 cm × 21.2 cm
4 1/2" × 4 1/2"	Squares: Cut 68.	11.2 cm × 11.2 cm

U.S.	ASSORTED SMALL-SCALE PRINTS	METRIC
2 1/2" × 2 1/2"	Squares: Cut 752.	6.2 cm × 6.2 cm

U.S.	YELLOW PRINT	METRIC
2 1/2" × 2 1/2"	Squares: Cut 168.	6.2 cm × 6.2 cm

U.S.	GREEN PRINT	METRIC
2 1/2" × 2 1/2"	Squares: Cut 168.	6.2 cm × 6.2 cm
2 1/4" × 336"	Binding: Cut on the straight of grain and double folded.	5.7 cm × 870 cm

Block Assembly

Note: This quilt uses a simple 4-Patch block to build 5 different 8 1/2" × 8 1/2" (21.2 cm × 21.2 cm) blocks.

1. Small 4-Patch: Use 416 assorted small-scale print squares to make the small 4-patch blocks as shown.

Make 104

16-Patch: Sew 4 small 4-Patch blocks together to make a 16-Patch block.

Make 14

2. 3/4 16-Patch: Sew 3 of the small 4-Patch blocks to 1 medium-scale print square to make 3/4 of a 16-Patch block as shown.

Make 6

3. Double 4-Patch: Sew 2 of the small 4-Patch blocks to 2 medium-scale print squares as shown.

Make 4

4. 1/4 16-Patch: Sew 1 of the small 4-Patch blocks to 1 medium-scale print square and 1 medium-scale print rectangle as shown.

Make 22

5. Large 4-Patch: Sew 4 medium-print squares to make a large 4-Patch block as shown.

Make 8

Quilt Assembly

Assemble 11 rows of 8 blocks. Follow the Quilt Assembly diagram or create your own block arrangement.

Top and Bottom Borders

1. Sew 16 yellow print squares alternately with 16 assorted small-scale print squares. Press seams toward the yellow print squares. Make 4 rows.

2. Sew 16 green print squares alternately with 16 assorted small-scale print squares. Press seams toward the green print squares. Make 4 rows.

3. Alternately sew 2 yellow print square rows to 2 green print square rows as shown. Make 2 of these border strips. Press.

4. Sew the border strips to the top and bottom edges of the quilt. Press.

Side Borders

1. Sew 26 yellow print squares alternately with 26 assorted small-scale print squares. Press seams toward the yellow print squares. Make 4 rows.

2. Sew 26 green print squares alternately with 26 assorted small-scale print squares. Press seams toward the green print squares. Make 4 rows.

3. Alternately sew the 2 yellow print square rows to 2 green print square rows. Make 2 of these border strips. Press.

4. Sew the border strips to the sides of the quilt and press.

Finishing

1. Layer and baste the quilt top with batting and backing.

2. Quilt a diagonal grid across the center field of the quilt

3. Stitch a button to the center of each yellow and green print square in the borders.

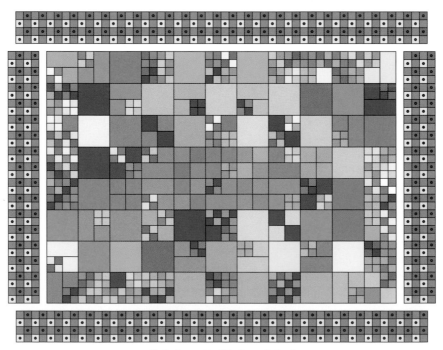
Quilt Assembly (Horizontal view)

Scrappy Holiday Bedside Rug

MADE BY: Reiko Washizawa
PHOTO BY: Akinori Miyashita
FINISHED SIZE: 30" × 42" (75 cm × 105 cm)
TECHNIQUES: Piecing/Appliqué

Don't little feet deserve a holiday treat, too? This Christmas rug is a wonderful accompaniment to the bed-size patchwork quilt, and an unusual twist on quilted fare.

PROJECT REQUIREMENTS

U.S.		METRIC
3/4 yard	Dark green print for squares and holly leaves	70 cm
3/4 yard	Medium-toned print for squares and binding	70 cm
1/4 yard	Yellow print for squares	20 cm
1/4 yard	Light green print for holly leaves	20 cm
1/8 yard	Red for holly berries	10 cm
1 yard	Tan for borders	90 cm
34" × 46"	Batting	85 cm × 115 cm
1 3/8 yards	Backing	1.2 meters

CUTTING

U.S.	DARK GREEN PRINT	METRIC
2 1/2" × 2 1/2"	Squares: Cut 40.	6.2 cm × 6.2 cm
Holly leaf template	Cut 32.	Holly leaf template

U.S.	MEDIUM-TONED PRINT	METRIC
2 1/2" × 2 1/2"	Squares: Cut 67.	6.2 cm × 6.2 cm
2 1/4" × 160"	Binding: Cut on the straight of grain and double folded.	5.7 cm × 400 cm

U.S.	YELLOW PRINT	METRIC
2 1/2" × 2 1/2"	Squares: Cut 28.	6.2 cm × 6.2 cm

U.S.	LIGHT GREEN PRINT	METRIC
Holly leaf template	Cut 12.	Holly leaf template

U.S.	RED	METRIC
Holly berry template	Cut 36.	Holly berry template

CUTTING CONTINUED

U.S.	TAN	METRIC
6³/4" x 30¹/2"	Top and bottom borders: Cut 2.	16.9 cm x 77.6 cm
6³/4" x 31¹/2"	Side borders: Cut 2.	16.9 cm x 78.8 cm

Project Assembly

1. Sew 8 dark green print squares alternately with 7 medium-toned print squares. Make 5 rows. Press seams toward the dark green print squares.

2. Sew 8 medium-toned print squares alternately with 7 yellow print squares. Make 4 rows. Press seams toward the yellow print squares.

3. Sew the dark green print rows alternately with the yellow print rows. Press.

4. Measure the rug horizontally through the center. Cut the top and bottom borders to this length. Sew the top and bottom borders to the rug. Press the seams toward the borders.

5. Measure the rug vertically through the center, including the top and bottom borders. Cut the side borders to this length and sew them to the rug. Press the seams toward the borders.

6. Arrange and stitch the holly leaves to the borders, allowing some leaves to overlap the seams.

7. Stitch along the outer edge of each berry and pull the stitches tight to gather. Secure with a knot. Stitch the berries to the borders.

8. Layer and baste the rug to the batting and backing.

9. Quilt in the ditch between the rows of squares and around the holly leaves and berries.

Rug Assembly

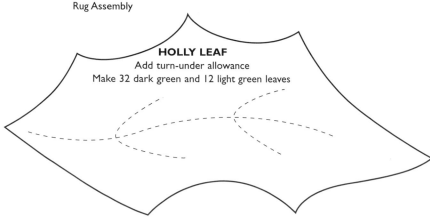

HOLLY BERRY

Do not add turn-under allowance

Make 36

HOLLY LEAF
Add turn-under allowance
Make 32 dark green and 12 light green leaves

Winter Scene Appliqué Pillow

MADE BY: Chieko Ishizaki
PHOTO BY: Norio Ando
FINISHED SIZE: 12" x 18" (30 cm x 45 cm)
TECHNIQUES: Appliqué

Make any number of these snowy landscape pillows from the templates included with this project. Adapt the templates to your own design or use them as pictured. For a short-cut to create the fencing, use ribbon or 1/4" (0.6 cm) bias tape.

PROJECT REQUIREMENTS

U.S.		METRIC
1/8 yard	Beige polka dot for sky	10 cm
1/4 yard	Cream for far hillside	15 cm
1/4 yard	White for near hillside	20 cm
3/4 yard, total	Assorted greens, brown plaids, and stripes for trees, fences, borders, and pillow back	70 cm, total
14" x 20"	Batting	35 cm x 50 cm
1/2 yard	Lining	45 cm
12" x 18"	Pillow form	30 cm x 45 cm

CUTTING

U.S.	BEIGE POLKA DOT	METRIC
3 1/2" x 15 1/2"	Sky: Cut 1.	8.7 cm x 38.8 cm

U.S.	CREAM	METRIC
4 1/2" x 15 1/2"	Far hillside: Cut 1.	11.2 cm x 38.8 cm

U.S.	WHITE	METRIC
6 1/2" X 15 1/2"	Near hillside: Cut 1.	16.2 cm x 38.8 cm

U.S.	GREENS, BROWN PLAIDS, AND STRIPES	METRIC
2" x 9 1/2"	Side borders: Cut 2.	5 cm x 23.4 cm
2" x 18 1/2"	Top and bottom borders: Cut 2.	5 cm x 46.2 cm
12 1/2" x 18 1/2"	Pillow back: Cut 1.	31.2 cm x 46.2 cm

Pillow Top Assembly

1. Cut wavy lines on 1 long side of the near and far hillside fabrics. Pin the far hillside to the sky fabric and then pin the near hillside in place as shown.

2. Cut out fencing, houses, trees, and snowdrifts. Arrange as desired and pin in place.

3. Begin with the background and appliqué using the method of your choice. Trim excess fabric from back.

4. Trim the appliquéd piece to measure 9¹/₂" x 15¹/₂" (10.2 cm x 38.7 cm).

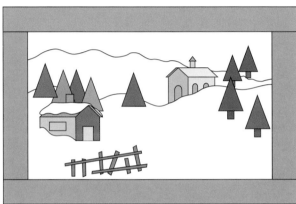

Pillow Top Assembly

Finishing

1. Sew the side borders to the pillow top. Press seams toward the borders.

2. Sew the top and bottom borders to the pillow top. Press seams toward the borders.

3. Layer and baste the pillow top with the batting and lining. Quilt the pillow top with wavy lines to indicate snowy hills.

4. Sew the pillow back to the pillow top, right sides together, leaving an opening for turning. Turn the pillow top right side out and press. Insert the pillow form and close the opening with hand stitches.

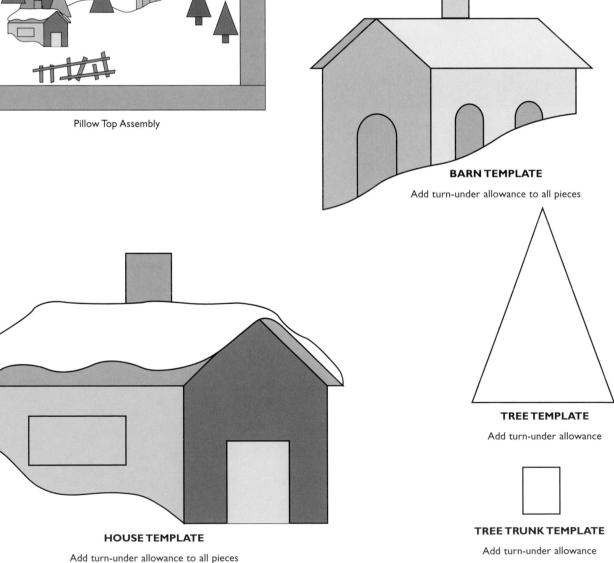

BARN TEMPLATE

Add turn-under allowance to all pieces

TREE TEMPLATE

Add turn-under allowance

TREE TRUNK TEMPLATE

Add turn-under allowance

HOUSE TEMPLATE

Add turn-under allowance to all pieces

Reindeer Redwork Pillow

MADE BY: Chieko Ishizaki
PHOTO BY: Norio Ando
FINISHED SIZE: 20¹/₂" x 22¹/₂" (52 cm x 57 cm)
TECHNIQUES: Paper piecing/Embroidery/Appliqué

Here's a small project with broad appeal to quilters. Use paper piecing, redwork embroidery, and appliqué to create this charming pillow. The trees on the original pillow are decorated with tiny appliquéd golden ovals (like glowing lanterns) and silvery-white triangles to mimic snow-laden branches. For construction ease, use printed green fabric to obtain a similar effect.

PROJECT REQUIREMENTS

U.S.		METRIC
2¹/₈ yards	White for background, borders, and back	1.9 meters
7" x 7" square	Tan for background of house block	18 cm x 18 cm square
Assorted scraps	Warm tones for paper piecing house and tree trunks*	Assorted scraps
3" x 24" rectangle	Solid green for tree tops	8 cm x 60 cm rectangle
¹/₄ yard	Green geometric for tree branches	25 cm
¹/₄ yard	Green dots for tree branches	25 cm
1 skein	Red embroidery floss	1 skein
⁵/₈ yard	Lining	60 cm
24" x 24"	Batting	65 cm x 65 cm
2¹/₂ yards	Packaged piping trim	2.3 meters
22" x 22"	Pillow form	55 cm x 55 cm
	Optional: Red beads for reindeer noses	

Refer to templates for color placement, or choose your own tones.

CUTTING

U.S.	WHITE	METRIC
2³/₄" x 11¹/₈"	Inner top and bottom borders: Cut 2.	6.7 cm x 28.2 cm
3¹/₄" x 9¹/₄"	Inner side borders: Cut 2.	8.3 cm x 23.2 cm
2¹/₈" x 23"	Outer top and bottom borders: Cut 2.	5.4 cm x 58.4 cm
2¹/₈" x 17³/₄"	Outer side borders: Cut 2.	5.4 cm x 45 cm
21" x 23"	Pillow back: Cut 1.	53.3 cm x 58 cm

U.S.	LINING	METRIC
25" x 27"	Cut 1.	64 cm x 70 cm

Christmas Cottage

1. Make 1 copy of House units 1–4 and follow the numbered sequence to complete the Christmas cottage. Choose your own colors or follow the color palette printed on the templates. Refer to the Paper Piecing Primer on page 8 for how-to instructions.

2. Make a pattern from the heart in House Unit 3. Cut a heart from red fabric, adding a turn-under allowance. Appliqué the heart to the cottage door.

Tree Block

Assemble Tree Units 1 and 2 to make the block. Make 16 tree blocks.

Pillow Assembly

1. Sew 1 tree to each side of the house block.

2. Sew the inner top and bottom borders to the house unit. Press toward the inner borders.

3. Sew the inner side borders to the house unit. Press toward the borders.

4. Assemble 7 trees in a horizontal row to make a tree border. Make 2 tree borders. Sew a tree border to the top and bottom of the pillow cover. Press seams toward the inner borders.

5. Sew the outer side borders to the pillow cover. Press seams toward the outer borders. Then sew the outer top and bottom borders to the pillow cover and press seams toward the outer borders.

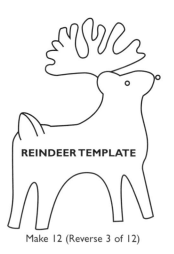

REINDEER TEMPLATE

Make 12 (Reverse 3 of 12)

Redwork Embroidery

1. Trace the reindeer outline onto the pillow cover. Evenly space 3 reindeer above and 3 below the house and 3 reindeer on each inner side border. Note that the reindeer on the right face the house.

2. Use a double strand of embroidery floss and a stem stitch to outline each reindeer.

Finishing the Pillow

1. Layer and baste the pillow top, batting, and lining. Quilt parallel horizontal lines, $3/8"$ (1 cm) apart, across the pillow cover. Trim the edges of the pillow top to straighten the sides and square the corners. Baste the piping to the pillow top with the raw edge of the piping toward the edge of the pillow, clipping the piping flange as needed to turn the corners.

2. Sew the pillow back to the pillow top, right sides together, leaving an opening for turning. Trim the corners and turn the pillow top right side out and press. Insert the pillow form and close the opening with hand stitches.

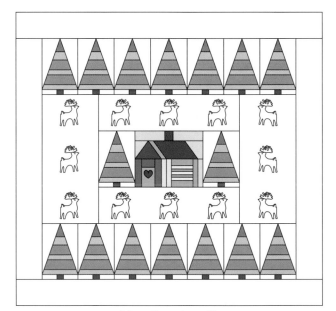

Pillow Cover Assembly

HOUSE UNIT 1

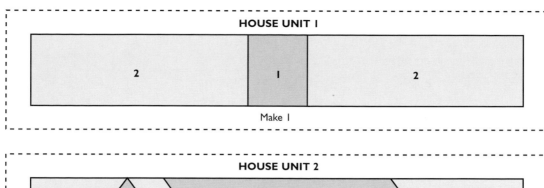

Make 1

HOUSE UNIT 2

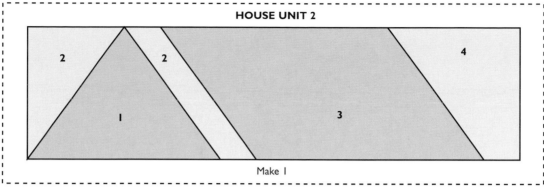

Make 1

HOUSE UNIT 3

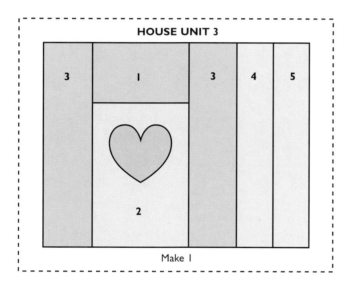

Make 1

HOUSE UNIT 4

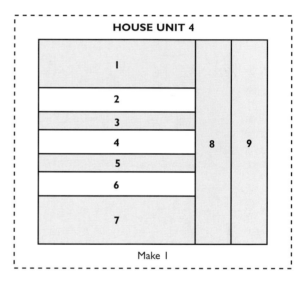

Make 1

TREE UNIT 1

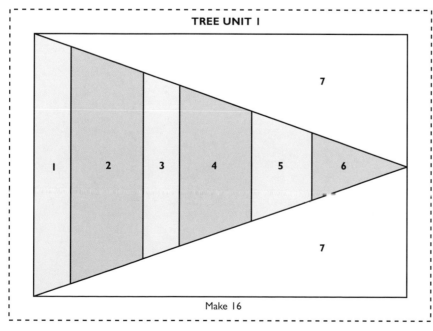

Make 16

TREE UNIT 2

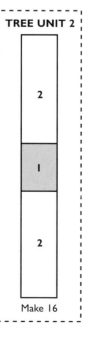

Make 16

Dancing Santas Quilt

Dancing Santas Quilt

MADE BY: Mayumi Hattori
PHOTO BY: Akinori Miyashita

FINISHED SIZE: 34³/8" × 34³/8" (87.3 cm × 87.3 cm)
FINISHED BLOCK SIZE: 5" × 5" (12.5 cm × 12.5 cm)
TECHNIQUES: Piecing/Paper piecing/Embroidery

In this quilt Santa dances to a Christmas beat—who can resist the joy of the jolly old gent as he celebrates another successful holiday? This upbeat wall hanging exemplifies the clever designs, great color use, and wonderful quilting that we associate with Japanese quiltmakers.

FABRIC REQUIREMENTS

U.S.		METRIC
¹/8 yard	Christmas print for star centers*	10 cm
¹/8 yard	Rust for star points	20 cm
¹/4 yard	Light print for star block corners	20 cm
1¹/8 yards	Medium blue for blocks and outer borders	1.2 meters
¹/4 yard	Red for Santa blocks	30 cm
¹/8 yard	Black for Santa blocks	20 cm
¹/8 yard	Flesh for Santa blocks	10 cm
¹/2 yard	White for Santa blocks	45 cm
¹/4 yard	Green for Santa blocks	20 cm
³/8 yard	Dark blue for inner borders and binding	35 cm
38" × 38"	Batting	95 cm × 95 cm
1¹/8 yards	Backing	1 meter
	Black embroidery floss for Santa eyes	
	Remember to purchase more yardage for fussy cut squares.	

CUTTING

U.S.	CHRISTMAS PRINT	METRIC
3" × 3"	Star centers: Cut 13.	7.5 cm × 7.5 cm

U.S.	RUST	METRIC
2¹/8" × 2¹/8"	Star points: Cut 52 squares. Cut squares in half diagonally.	5.3 cm × 5.3 cm

U.S.	LIGHT PRINT	METRIC
1³/4" × 1³/4"	Star block corners: Cut 52.	4.3 cm × 4.3 cm

U.S.	MEDIUM BLUE	METRIC
3³/4" × 3³/4"	Star sides: Cut 13 squares. Cut squares into quarters diagonally.	9.4 cm × 9.4 cm
2³/4" × 2³/4"	Santa setting triangles: Cut 48 squares. Cut squares in half diagonally.	5.3 cm × 5.3 cm
4¹/2" × 26"	Outer top and bottom borders: Cut 2.	11.2 cm × 64.7 cm
4¹/2" × 34"	Outer side borders: Cut 2.	11.2 cm × 84.7 cm

U.S.	GREEN	METRIC
1³/₄" x 1³/₄"	Santa block corners: Cut 48.	4.3 cm x 4.3 cm

U.S.	DARK BLUE	METRIC
¹/₂" x 25¹/₂"	Inner top and bottom borders: Cut 2.	1.2 cm x 63.7 cm
¹/₂" x 26"	Inner side borders: Cut 2.	1.2 cm x 64.7 cm
2¹/₄" x 138"	Binding: Cut on the straight of grain and double folded.	5.7 cm x 340 cm
38" x 38"	Backing	95 cm x 95 cm

Sawtooth Star Block

1. Sew 1 rust triangle to each short side of a medium-blue triangle to a make a star-point unit. Press the seams toward the rust triangles. Make 52 units.

2. Sew 1 light print corner square to each side of 26 star-point units to make star-side units. Press the seams toward the corner squares.

3. Sew 1 star-point unit to each side of a star-center square. Press the seams toward the center square. Make 13 units.

4. Sew the star side units to the star center units. Press. Make 13 Sawtooth star blocks.

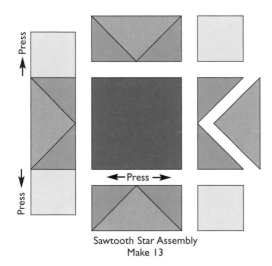

Sawtooth Star Assembly
Make 13

Paper Piecing Santas

1. Paper piecing is a fast and accurate method for piecing blocks with very small units. See the Paper Piecing Primer on page 8 for instructions. Make 12 photocopies of the 6 Santa units. Follow the colored and numbered sequences to finish each unit.

2. Sew completed Santa Units 2 and 2r to a completed Santa Unit 1.

3. Sew completed Santa Units 4 and 4r to a completed Santa Unit 3.

4. Sew the 2 resulting Units to make 1 Santa. Make 12 Dancing Santas.

5. Sew 1 medium-blue triangle to each of 2 adjacent sides of a green corner square. Press seams toward the triangles. Make 48 corner units.

6. Sew 4 corner units to each Santa.

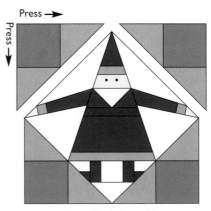

Santa Block Assembly
Make 12

Quilt Assembly

1. Refer to the assembly diagram for placement of Santa blocks. Note: The Santa blocks rotate randomly across the quilt top.

2. Sew 3 rows with 3 Star blocks and 2 Santa blocks.

3. Sew 2 rows with 3 Santa blocks and 2 Star blocks.

4. Sew the rows together alternately as shown.

Borders

1. Measure the quilt horizontally through the center and cut 2 inner borders to this length. Sew the top and bottom inner borders to the quilt top. Press toward the borders.

2. Measure the quilt top vertically through the center, including the top and bottom inner borders. Cut 2 inner borders to this length. Sew the side inner borders to the quilt top. Press toward the inner borders.

3. Repeat for the outer borders.

Finishing

1. Use the black floss to embroider Santa's eyes.

2. Layer the quilt top with the batting and backing. Quilt a diagonal grid in the center field of the quilt. Quilt random stars and double wavy lines in the outer border.

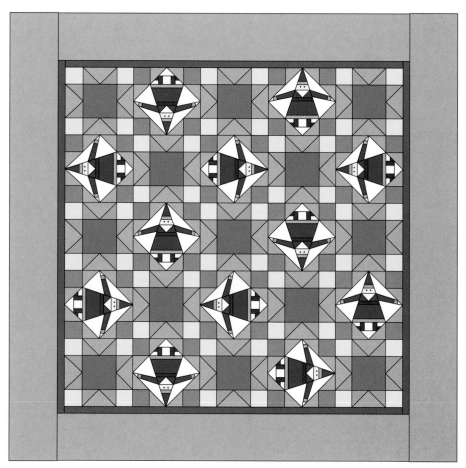

Quilt Assembly

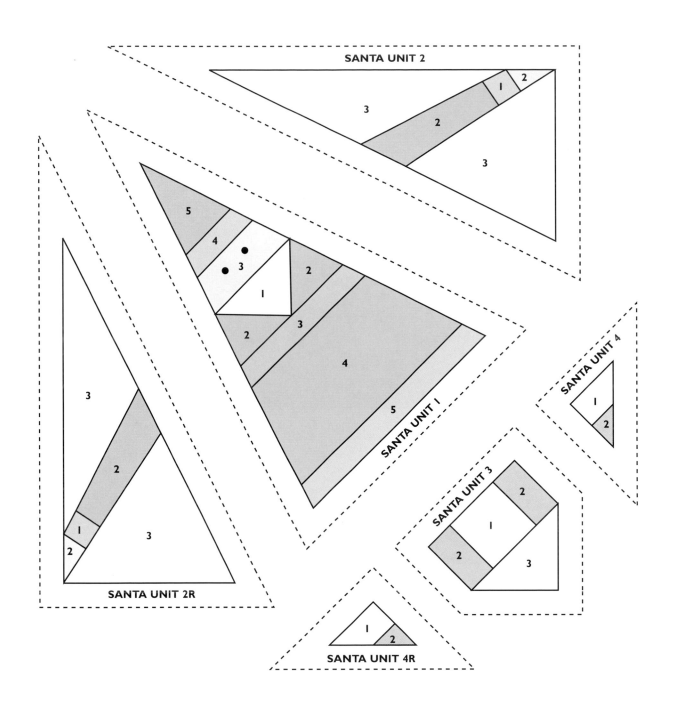

SANTA UNITS: Make 12 of each

Angel Ornament & Garland

MADE BY: Chieko Ishizaki
PHOTO BY: Norio Ando
FINISHED SIZE: 5 1/4" × 5" (13 cm × 15 cm)
TECHNIQUES: Piecing/Embroidery/Beading

Create your own heavenly choir with this sweet little ornament pattern. Make pretty accents for your tree or string a chorus line together for a charming decorative garland.

PROJECT REQUIREMENTS

U.S.		METRIC
10" × 10"	Muslin for body and arms	25 cm × 25 cm
7" × 14"	Calico for dress	18 cm × 35 cm
7" × 14"	Calico for dress lining	18 cm × 35 cm
6" × 15"	White sateen for wings and heart or star	15 cm × 38 cm
1/4 yard	Yarn for hair	25 cm
1/4 yard	1/4" (0.6 cm) Ribbon for bows	25 cm
1/4 yard	3/8" (0.8 cm) Ribbon for hanger	25 cm
7" × 4"	Very lightweight interfacing for wings	17.5 cm × 10 cm
2	Star sequins	2
3 dozen	2 mm gold beads	3 dozen
	Black and red embroidery floss for facial features	
	Polyester filling	

Note: As the fabric requirements for this project are very small, we've listed the amounts as fabric pieces rather than as purchased yardage. This project will yield 1 angel, increase yardage as needed for more. Also, embellish the angels to suit your taste—take advantage of the many wonderful trims and baubles available to dress up your angel.

Angel Body

1. Sew the body front to the body back leaving the shoulders between the marked dots and the bottom edge unsewn. Clip curves. Turn to the right side.

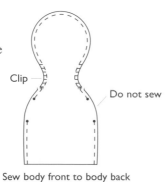

Sew body front to body back

2. Sew 2 arms, right sides together. Clip the angle between thumb and fingers. Turn to the right side. Make 2.

3. Stuff arms tightly with filling and then close the opening.

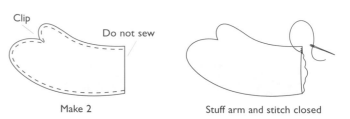

Make 2

Stuff arm and stitch closed

4. Insert the arms into the shoulder openings with the thumbs upward. Close the shoulder seams, making sure to catch the arms in those seams.

5. Stuff the head and body tightly with filling and then close the opening at the bottom.

Finishing the body

Angel Dress

1. Sew a dress front to a dress back, leaving the armholes unsewn between the dots. Repeat for the lining.

Do not sew   Do not sew

Clip

Sew dress to lining

2. Press the seams open. Turn the lining to the right side and insert it into the dress so that the right side of the lining is facing the right side of the dress. Sew the dress to the lining at the neck and the hem. Clip corners.

3. Turn the lined dress right side out through 1 armhole. Press. Turn the raw edges of the dress and lining in and stitch to finish the armholes.

Stitch dress to lining at armholes

4. Place the dress over the angel's head and pull the arms through the armholes.

Angel Wings

1. Place the wings right sides together with the interfacing on the wrong side of 1 wing. Sew all 3 pieces together, leaving a space unsewn between the marked dots for turning. Clip the "V" between the wings and trim the interfacing very close to the seam.

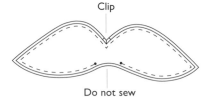

Clip

Do not sew

2. Turn the wings right side out and press. Close the opening with hand stitches. Embellish the wings with the sequins and beads.

Finishing the wings

Adding Decorative Hearts or Stars

1. Sew the hearts (or stars) right sides together. Leave a space unsewn between the marked dots for turning. Clip into the "V" of the heart (or star).

Clip

Do not sew

Sew heart

2. Stuff the heart (or star) with filling and stitch the opening closed. Stitch a bow to the front of the heart.

Finishing the heart

Finishing Angel Ornament

1. Stitch the wings to the back of the angel.

2. Bring the angel's arms to the front and stitch 1 hand to each side of the heart (or star).

3. Cut short lengths of the yarn and stitch it to the angel's head. Stitch a bow to the hair.

4. Make a loop with the hanger ribbon and stitch it to the wings.

Finishing Angel Garland

1. Make 5 angels, leaving arms outspread, and appliqué a heart to the front of each dress. (Refer to page 3 for the project photo.)

2. Make 6 stuffed hearts and embellish them with beads and star sequins.

3. Alternately stitch hearts to angel hands to make the garland. Stitch a length of ribbon to each end of the garland for easier display.

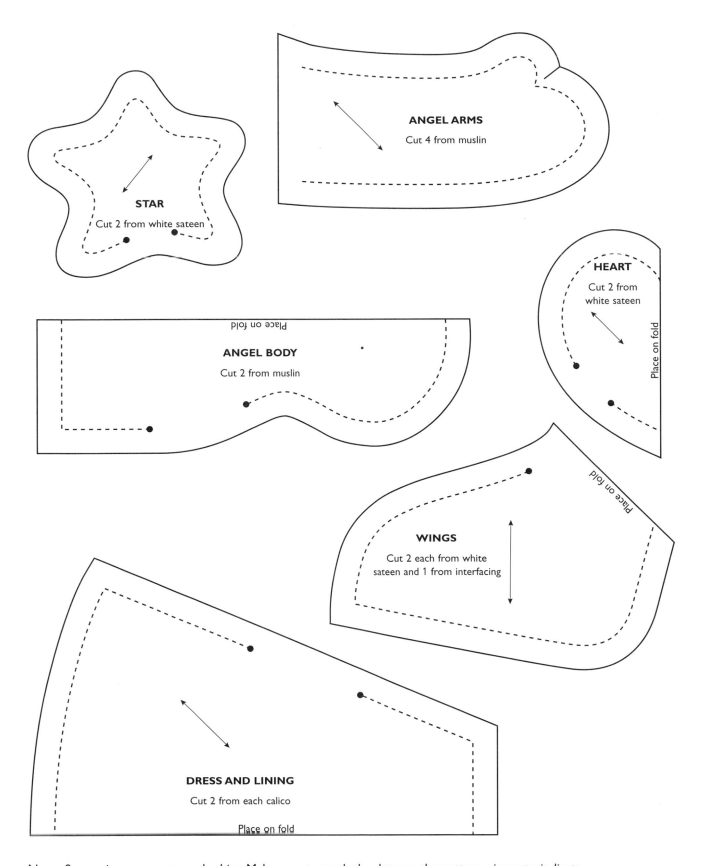

STAR

Cut 2 from white sateen

ANGEL ARMS

Cut 4 from muslin

HEART

Cut 2 from white sateen

Place on fold

ANGEL BODY

Cut 2 from muslin

Place on fold

WINGS

Cut 2 each from white sateen and 1 from interfacing

Place on fold

DRESS AND LINING

Cut 2 from each calico

Place on fold

Note: Some pieces are cut on the bias. Make sure to mark the dots on the pattern pieces to indicate unsewn seams. Trace the angel body onto the muslin and transfer the facial features. Embroider the angel's face before cutting out the body front.

Christmas Boxes Quilt

Christmas Boxes Quilt
MADE BY: Yoshie Ishiguro
PHOTO BY: Norio Ando

FINISHED SIZE: 68½" × 93¼" (174 cm × 237 cm)
FINISHED BLOCK SIZE: 4¾" × 8" (12.1 cm × 20.7 cm)
TECHNIQUES: Piecing/Y-seams/Embellishments

What could be better than stacks of beribboned and bedecked presents under a Christmas tree? This quilt is certainly challenging with Y-seaming and inset decorative accents, but the final result is a dazzling heirloom quilt to be treasured for generations.

FABRIC REQUIREMENTS

U.S.		METRIC
3 yards	A variety of dark prints for boxes and outer border	2.7 meters
2¾ yards	A variety of medium prints for boxes and outer border	2.5 meters
2¾ yards	A variety of light prints for boxes	2.5 meters
2⅝ yards	Alternate light print for inner and pieced borders and binding	2.4 meters
1¼ yards	Red for boxes and bows	1 meter
5½ yards	Backing	5 meters
74" × 99"	Batting	184 cm × 247 cm

CUTTING

U.S.	DARK PRINTS	METRIC
2⅛" wide	Diamonds: Cut 36 strips.	5.4 cm wide
Template A/Ar*	Star points: Cut 10 and 10r.	Template A/Ar
Template B/Br	Star points: Cut 10 and 10r.	Template B/Br
Template G	Outer border: Cut 80.	Template G

*Reminder: The "r" means a reversed template.

U.S.	MEDIUM PRINTS	METRIC
2⅛" wide	Diamonds: Cut 32 strips.	5.4 cm wide
Template G	Outer border: Cut 80.	Template G
Template C/Cr	Star background: Cut 10 and 10r.	Template C/Cr

U.S.	LIGHT PRINTS	METRIC
2⅛" wide	Diamonds: Cut 36 strips.	5.4 cm wide
Template E	Horizontal half-diamond: Cut 36.	Template E
Template F	Vertical half-diamond: Cut 30.	Template F

U.S.	RED	METRIC
2⅛" wide	Diamonds: Cut 1 strip.	5.4 cm wide
Template D/Dr	Pieced bows: Cut 12 and 6r.	Template D/Dr
3¾" × 30"	Bows: Cut 6.	9.5 cm × 75 cm

U.S.	ALTERNATE LIGHT PRINT	METRIC
Template G	Outer border: Cut 156.	Template G
5" x 79¹/₄"	Side inner border: Cut 2.	12.2 cm x 208.2 cm
5" x 66¹/₂"	Top and bottom inner border: Cut 2.	12.2 cm x 166 cm
2¹/₄" x 340"	Binding: Cut on the straight of grain and double folded.	5.7 cm x 852 cm

Note: The center field of this quilt consists of 49 pieced box blocks. Each box is made up of 60° pieced diamonds sewn from dark, medium, and light colored fabrics. Of the boxes, 5 boxes have a star pieced into 1 side and 6 are pieced to resemble ribbon-tied boxes with three-dimensional bows. There are also 22 partial boxes to fill out the top, bottom, and sides of the center field.

Cutting Diamonds from Strips

Use the 60° angle on a rotary ruler to sub-cut each strip into individual diamonds, 2³/₈" (6 cm) apart. Keep the diamonds arranged by color value. Most will form the pieced diamond sets, but there will be leftover diamonds for the bow-tied and star-studded boxes.

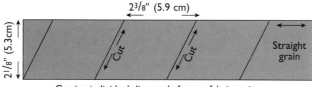

Cutting individual diamonds from a fabric strip

Cut 36 strips for dark colored diamonds, 32 strips for medium colored diamonds, 36 strips for light colored diamonds, and 1 red strip for bow-tied boxes

Assembly of Christmas Boxes

1. Each box has 3 sides: a light colored top, a medium colored left side, and a dark colored right side.

2. Sew 9 diamonds together to make 1 side of a box.

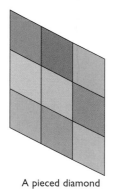

A pieced diamond

Make 43 dark, 38 medium, 43 light pieced diamonds

3. Take 1 dark, medium, and light pieced diamond to make a complete box. Sew 3 pieced diamonds together by first sewing the seam between the left and right sides of the box (the medium and dark pieced diamonds). Stop sewing ¹/₄" (0.6 cm) away from the top of the seam. Sew the top of the box (the light-pieced diamond) to the sides of the box by sewing ¹/₄" (0.6 cm) away from the inner point to the right side of the box and then ¹/₄" (0.6 cm) away from the inner point to the left side of the box. Do not press the seams until indicated in later sections. Make 38 boxes.

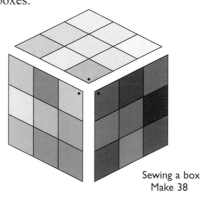

Sewing a box
Make 38

Assembly of Bow-tied Christmas Boxes

Important: Note the orientation of the red bow strip when sewing the block.

1. Make 2 strips of 3 medium diamonds and 2 strips of 3 dark diamonds for the sides of each box. Make a total of 12 medium diamond strips and 12 dark diamond strips.

2. Sew a medium diamond strip to either side of a red bow strip to make the left side of the bow-tied box. Press. Make 6 units.

3. Sew a dark diamond strip to either side of a red bow strip to make the right side of the bow-tied box. Press. Make 6 units.

4. To make the box top, sew a light diamond to either side of a red diamond. Press. Sew these units to each side of a red bow strip. Press. Make 6 box top units.

5. Assemble the bow-tied boxes in the same manner as the plain boxes. Again, wait to press the seams. (Bow embellishment to be added later.)

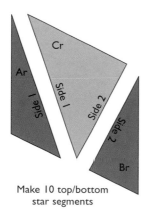

Make 6 bow-tied boxes

Assembly of Star-studded Christmas Boxes

Use the remaining light pieced diamonds and dark pieced diamonds for the top and right sides of the star-studded boxes. Use 4 medium diamonds for the star corners and 1 dark diamond for the star center.
Important: Note the orientation of the templates for the points of the star when sewing the block.

1. To make the top and bottom star segments sew side 1 of Ar to side 1 of Cr. Sew side 2 of Br to side 2 of Cr. Make 10 segments.

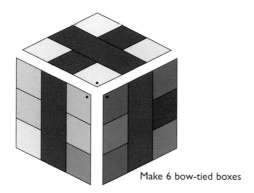

Make 10 top/bottom
star segments

2. Sew a medium diamond to each side of the top/bottom star segments. Press toward the diamonds.

3. To make the right and left star segments sew side 1 of A to side 1 of C. Sew side 2 of B to side 2 of C. Make 10 segments.

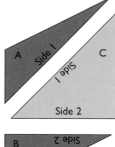

Make 10 right/left
star segments

4. Sew a right/left star segment to each side of a dark diamond. Press toward the diamond. Make 5 stars.

5. Assemble the 5 star-studded boxes in the same manner as the other boxes. Again, wait to press the seams.

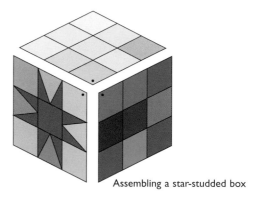

Assembling a star-studded box

Assembly of Horizontal Pieced Half-Diamonds

1. Use 3 light diamonds cut from a strip and 3 light horizontal half-diamonds made from the template to make each of the horizontal pieced half-diamonds for the top and bottom of the quilt's center field.

2. Sew the light diamonds to the horizontal half-diamonds. Press. Make 12.

Make 12 horizontal pieced half-diamonds

Assembly of Partial Box Blocks

1. Use 1 medium pieced diamond, 1 dark pieced diamond, and 1 horizontal pieced half-diamond for each partial box block.

2. Assemble the partial boxes in the same manner as the complete box blocks. Press. Make 6.

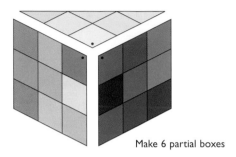

Make 6 partial boxes

Assembly of Vertical Pieced Half-Diamonds

1. Use 3 light-colored diamonds cut from a strip and 3 light-colored vertical half-diamonds made from the template to make the vertical pieced half-diamond units for the sides of the quilt's center field.

2. Sew the light colored diamonds to the vertical half-diamonds. Press. Make 10.

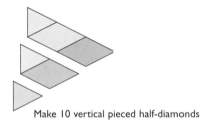

Make 10 vertical pieced half-diamonds

Assembly of Right and Left Half-Box Blocks

1. Make 5 half-box blocks for the left side of the quilt using a dark pieced diamond and a vertical half–diamond unit.

Make 5 left-side half-box blocks

2. Make 5 half-box blocks for the right side of the quilt using a medium pieced diamond and a vertical half–diamond unit.

Make 5 right-side
half-box blocks

Quilt Assembly

Note: A design wall will be very helpful in laying out the boxes and creating a random arrangement of the star-studded and bow-tied boxes.

1. Sew 6 partial box blocks together to make the top row of the center field of the quilt, making sure to leave 1/4" (0.6 cm) unsewn at the ends of the seams between each box. Press the seams open.

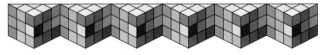

Make 1 top row

2. Make 5 rows with 5 complete boxes, 1 left-side box, and 1 right-side box. Start and stop sewing 1/4" (0.6 cm) from the ends of the seams. Press the seams open.

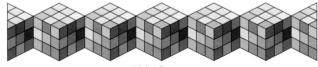

Make 5 rows

3. Make 4 rows with 6 complete boxes. Start and stop sewing 1/4" (0.6 cm) from the ends of the seams. Press the seams open.

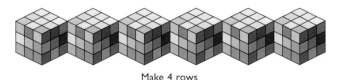

Make 4 rows

4. Assemble the center field of the quilt top by alternating the 4 rows with 6 complete boxes with the 5 rows with 5 complete boxes and 2 side boxes. Sew the top row to the center field.

5. Sew the 6 remaining horizontal half-diamonds to the bottom row of boxes. Press.

Border Assembly

1. Measure the quilt top vertically through the center and cut the 2 inner side borders to this length. Sew these borders to the sides of the quilt top. Press the seams toward the borders.

2. Measure the quilt top horizontally through the center, including the side borders, and cut the inner top and bottom borders to this length. Sew these borders to the quilt top. Press the seams toward the borders.

3. Alternately sew 46 medium and dark triangles to 45 border-print triangles to make each outer side border.

4. Alternately sew 34 medium and dark triangles to 33 border print triangles to make the outer top and bottom borders.

5. Pin and sew the outer borders to the quilt top, starting and stopping the seam $1/4$" (0.6 cm) away from each end.

6. Sew from the inner corner of the triangle borders to the outer corners to finish attaching the borders. Keep the corner of the inner border out of the way when sewing this last seam.

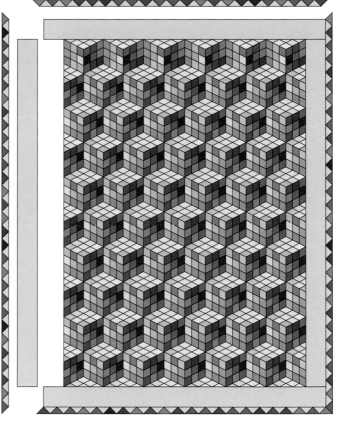

Adding outer borders

Finishing the Quilt

1. Layer and baste the quilt top, batting, and backing.

2. Quilt $1/4$" (0.6 cm) within each diamond in the center field of the quilt and within the pieced outer border. Quilt parallel lines, $1^{1}/4$" (3 cm) apart, along the inner borders.

3. With right sides together, sew each bow-tie along 1 short side and 1 long side. Trim the sewn corners and turn the bow-tie right side out. Press. Tie into a bow and stitch to the quilt.

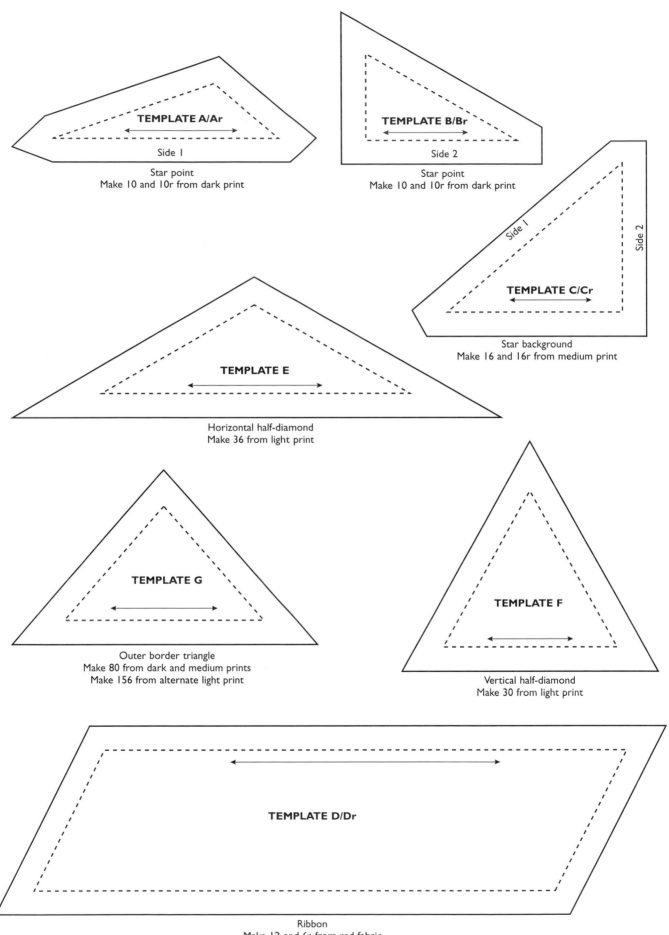

TEMPLATE A/Ar

Side 1

Star point
Make 10 and 10r from dark print

TEMPLATE B/Br

Side 2

Star point
Make 10 and 10r from dark print

Side 1

Side 2

TEMPLATE C/Cr

Star background
Make 16 and 16r from medium print

TEMPLATE E

Horizontal half-diamond
Make 36 from light print

TEMPLATE G

Outer border triangle
Make 80 from dark and medium prints
Make 156 from alternate light print

TEMPLATE F

Vertical half-diamond
Make 30 from light print

TEMPLATE D/Dr

Ribbon
Make 12 and 6r from red fabric

Braided Christmas Wreath

MADE BY: Mayumi Makino
PHOTO BY: Norio Ando
FINISHED SIZE: 12" (30 cm) diameter
TECHNIQUES: Fabric folding

Here's another entry for the hostess/teacher gift category—a simple and attractive fabric wreath. For quick holiday décor, especially for a busy teacher, hang the wreath on a doorknob or in a window. Another attractive option: encircle softly glowing candles.

PROJECT REQUIREMENTS

U.S.		METRIC
5/8 yard	Light Christmas print for wreath and wreath holder	60 cm
1/4 yard	Bright print for petals	20 cm
1/8 yard	Green print for leaves	10 cm
Scraps	Red solid for flower centers	Scraps
5 3/4 yards	1" (2.5 cm) piping filler	5.2 meters
1/4 yard	Ribbon to hang wreath	10 cm
	Template material for flower center pattern	

CUTTING

U.S.	LIGHT CHRISTMAS PRINT	METRIC
2 7/8" x 68"	Braids for wreath: Cut 3.	7 cm x 170 cm
3 5/8" x 5 1/2"	Wreath holder: Cut 1.	9 cm x 14 cm

U.S.	BRIGHT PRINT FOR PETALS	METRIC
3 1/4" x 3 1/4"	Cut 24.	8 cm x 8 cm

U.S.	GREEN PRINT FOR LEAVES	METRIC
3 1/4" x 3 1/4"	Cut 8.	8 cm x 8 cm

U.S.	FLOWER CENTERS	METRIC
Flower center template	Cut 4.	Flower center template

U.S.	PIPING FILLER FOR BRAID	METRIC
67"	Cut 3.	167.5 cm

Project Assembly

1. Fold the 3 braid strips in half lengthwise, right sides together. Sew their long sides and then turn each strip right side out.

2. Use a bodkin to pull a length of piping filler through each braid strip. Filler will not quite reach the ends of the braid strips.

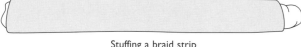

Stuffing a braid strip

Make 3

3. Turn the raw ends of each filled braid strip in ¹⁄₄" (0.6 cm). Pin the 3 braid strips together at one end. Braid the 3 strips tightly. Hand stitch the free ends of the braid to the pinned ends, keeping the raw edges tucked inside.

4. Fold the wreath holder in half crosswise, right sides together, and sew. Turn to the right side. Press.

5. Make a loop from the ribbon and sew to the center of the wreath holder 1" (2.5 cm) from 1 raw edge. Place the wreath wrong side up on the wreath holder with the ribbon loop at the top.

Stitched ends of braided wreath, wreath holder, and ribbon

6. Fold the ends of the wreath holder to the back of the wreath covering the braid ends. Stitch securely through the wreath holder and into the wreath.

Stitched ends of wreath holder

7. Fold the petals and leaves in half diagonally, wrong sides together. Fold in half diagonally again, bringing all the raw edges together.

First fold of petal and leaf   Second fold of petal and leaf

Hand stitch across the raw edge. Make a petal or leaf by pulling up the gathering threads, then secure with a knot.

Gathering petal and leaf

8. Arrange and stitch 6 petals to make 1 flower.

Petal arrangement

9. Hand stitch around the right side of each flower center ¹⁄₈" (0.3 cm) from the edge. Make a yo-yo by gathering up the stitches, securing them with a knot.

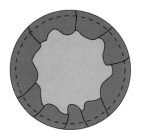 

FLOWER CENTER TEMPLATE

Cut 4

Stitched flower center

10. Stitch a flower center to the gathered petals. Stitch 2 leaves to the back of each flower. Stitch the flowers to the wreath. Be sure to cover the wreath holder with a flower.

Wreath

Pinecone Party Favor

MADE BY: Mayumi Makino
PHOTO BY: Norio Ando
FINISHED SIZE: 3⁷/₈" × 4⁷/₈" (9.5 cm × 12 cm)
TECHNIQUES: Fabric folding

There's nothing like holiday entertaining to strain the creativity of the hostess-gift giver. Baked goods and spirits are great, but here's a variation that is both unusual and pretty. This handmade fabric pinecone will dress up a table top or a mantel with an unusual seasonal accent.

PROJECT REQUIREMENTS

U.S.		METRIC
5" x 5"	Muslin	12 cm x 12 cm
3/8 yard	Christmas print for pinecone scales	25 cm
4" x 6"	Green print for leaf	10 cm x 15 cm
3/8 yard	1/4" (0.6 cm) wide ribbon	35 cm
Template material to make patterns for pinecone core, base, and leaf		
Small amount of stuffing for pinecone core and a small amount of batting for leaf		

CUTTING

U.S.	MUSLIN	METRIC
Pinecone core template	Cut 2.	Pinecone core template

U.S.	CHRISTMAS PRINT	METRIC
2¹/₂" x 2¹/₂"	Top of pinecone and small scales: Cut 28 squares.	6 cm x 6 cm
3¹/₄" x 3¹/₄"	Large pinecone scales: Cut 5 squares.	8 cm x 8 cm
Pinecone base template	Cut 1.	Pinecone base template

U.S.	GREEN PRINT	METRIC
Leaf template	Cut 2.	Leaf template

U.S.	BATTING	METRIC
Leaf template	Cut 1.	Leaf template

Project Assembly

1. Trace the templates to make patterns for the pinecone core, base, and leaf.

2. Cut 2 pinecone cores from muslin using the template.

3. Place the pinecone core pieces right sides together and sew along the long sides, leaving the bottom opening unstitched. Turn right side out. Stitch a line of basting along the opening of the pinecone core; do not cut the thread. Firmly stuff the pinecone core. Pull the basting thread tight and secure with a knot.

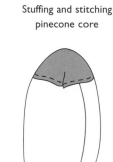

Stuffing and stitching pinecone core

4. Place and stitch the pinecone top over the tip of the pinecone core.

5. Fold and press each pinecone scale square in half. Fold the sides of each scale diagonally to meet in the center. Press.

Folding pinecone scale   Second fold of pinecone scale

6. With the folded side facing outward, place and stitch the scales to the pinecone core, starting at the top and working in rows around the pinecone.

Stitching pinecone scales to core

7. In the first row, stitch 4 small scales; in the second and third rows stitch 6 small scales; in the fourth row stitch 5 small scales; in the fifth row stitch 6 small scales; and in the sixth row, stitch 5 large scales. Stagger the placement of the scales from row to row.

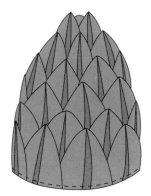

Pinecone scales stitched to core

8. Place the leaf pieces right sides together. Place a batting leaf on 1 side of this unit and sew through all layers, leaving an opening at the base of the leaf for turning. Trim the batting very close to the sewing line. Clip inside corners.

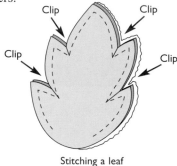

Stitching a leaf

9. Turn the leaf right side out. Close the opening with hand stitches. Quilt the leaf as shown.

10. Turn and baste the edges of the pinecone base to the wrong side along the indicated line.

Preparing pinecone base

11. Pin the leaf to the bottom of the pinecone. Place the pinecone base over the leaf and stitch through all layers to secure the base and leaf to the pinecone.

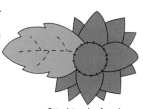

Stitching leaf and base to pinecone

12. Tie a bow with the ribbon and stitch it to the leaf.

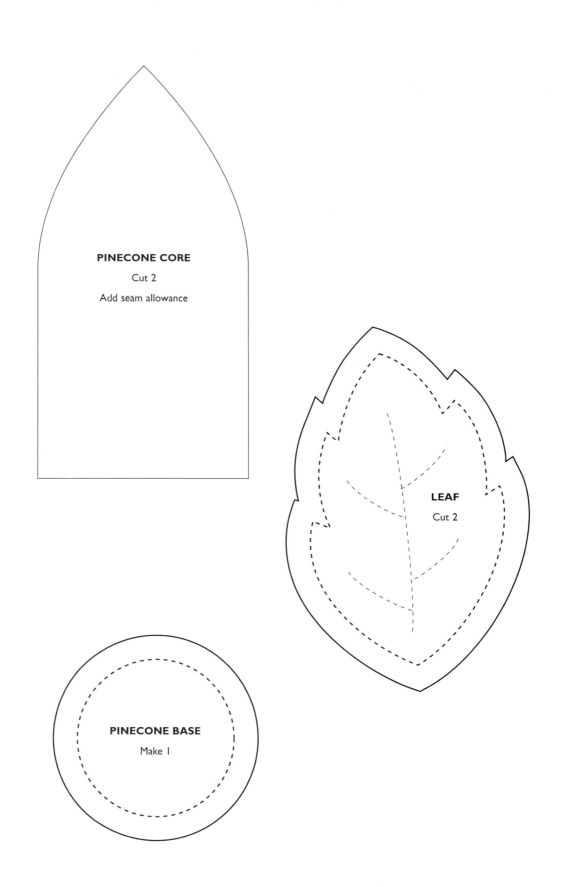

PINECONE CORE

Cut 2

Add seam allowance

LEAF

Cut 2

PINECONE BASE

Make 1

Star-Lit Christmas Tree Quilt

Star-Lit Christmas Tree Quilt
MADE BY: Fusako Inukai
PHOTO BY: Norio Ando

FINISHED SIZE: 55⅝" × 66½" (141.3 cm × 168.9 cm)
FINISHED BLOCK SIZE: 7¼" × 7¼" (18.4 cm × 18.4 cm)
TECHNIQUES: Piecing/Appliqué

Imagine a snowy Christmas night with a sparkling Christmas tree sitting in a blanket of snow—it's an image that translates wonderfully to other cultures. This quilting craftswoman has blended a few of our favorite Christmas themes to create an innovative masterpiece of traditional quiltmaking. A faithful recreation of this quilt will take time and skill, but there are shortcuts for those who'd like capture the feeling of the quilt without taking on such a challenging project. The patchwork Christmas tree can easily be cut from a scrap quilt, orphan blocks, or even Christmas-themed fabric. Instead of the feathered stars, use your own favorite star blocks.

FABRIC REQUIREMENTS

U.S.		METRIC
3 yards	Cream for background	2.7 meters
2 ½ yards, total	Assorted red and green prints for tree and star blocks	2.3 meters, total
⅜ yard	Yellow for feathered and treetop stars	35 cm
½ yard, total	Assorted brown prints for tree trunk, tree base, and holly vine	45 cm, total
¼ yard, total	Medium and dark greens for holly leaves	25 cm, total
⅛ yard	Red for holly berries	15 cm
1¾ yards	Light green for border and binding	1.6 meters
1 yard	White for snowballs	95 cm
4 yards	Backing	3.7 meters
58" x 71"	Batting	145 cm x 175 cm

CUTTING

U.S.	CREAM	METRIC
36½" x 44"	Tree background: Cut 1.	93.3 cm x 111.8 cm
Note: Consider cutting this piece slightly larger and then trimming to size before attaching the stars.		
3" x 15½"	Tree trunk strip: Cut 2.	7.6 cm x 39.4 cm
2" x 11"	Tree base strip: Cut 2.	5.1 cm x 28 cm
3¾" x 36¾"	Lower background border: Cut 1.	9.5 cm x 93.3 cm
4⅛" x 58½"	Side holly vine border: Cut 1.	10.2 cm x 148.6 cm
Template A/Ar	Star setting units: Cut 52 and 52r.	Template A/Ar
2" x 2"	Feathered star corner squares: Cut 52.	5.1 cm x 5.1 cm
2¼" x 2¼"	Star side triangles: Cut 13 squares. Cut squares diagonally into quarters.	5.7 cm x 5.7 cm

U.S.	ASSORTED RED AND GREEN PRINTS	METRIC
1" wide	Star diamonds: Cut 40 strips.	2.5 cm wide

U.S.	YELLOW	METRIC
1" wide	Star diamonds: Cut 8 strips.	2.5 cm wide
Template B	Treetop star points: Cut 5.	Template B
Template C	Treetop star center: Cut 1.	Template C

U.S.	**BROWN PRINT**	METRIC
2" x 16½"	Base of tree: Cut 1.	5.1 cm x 41.9 cm
1" x 190"	Holly vine: Cut on the bias.	2.5 cm x 490 cm

U.S.	**MEDIUM AND DARK GREEN PRINTS**	METRIC
Template D	Holly leaf: Cut 60.	Template D

U.S.	**RED**	METRIC
Template E	Holly berry: Cut 60.	Template E

U.S.	**LIGHT GREEN FOR OUTER BORDERS**	METRIC
4½" x 58½"	Side borders: Cut 2.	11.4 cm x 148.6 cm
4½" x 55⅝"	Top and bottom borders: Cut 2.	11.4 cm x 141.3 cm
2¼" x 260"	Binding: Cut on the straight of grain and double folded.	5.7 cm x 660 cm

U.S.	**WHITE FOR SNOWBALLS**	METRIC
Template F	Cut 190, total.	Template F

U.S.	**BACKING**	METRIC
60" x 71"	Make 1.	152 cm x 180 cm

Christmas Tree

1. Arrange assorted blocks and strips of fabric into a triangle that is approximately 30" (76 cm) wide at its base and 35" (89 cm) tall. Match the center of each strip to the center of the strip to which it is being sewn. Press.

2. Pin and appliqué the Christmas tree to the background centered horizontally and aligned at the lower edge. You may elect to trim away the background behind the tree once it is appliquéd in place. Press.

Strip-pieced Christmas tree

3. Cut and sew assorted brown fabrics into a rectangle to measure 3" x 6½" (7.6 cm x 15.9 cm). Sew a tree trunk background to each side of the tree trunk. Press seams toward the backgrounds. Center and sew the tree trunk strip to the bottom of the Christmas tree.

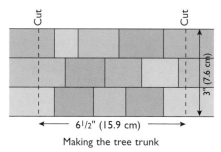

Making the tree trunk

4. Cut outward curves into the short sides of the tree base. Appliqué each side of the tree base to a tree base background. Press seams toward the tree base. Trim the tree base strip to measure 36¾" (93.3 cm) wide. Center and sew the tree base strip to the tree trunk strip.

5. Sew the lower background border to the tree base strip. Press seam toward the lower background border.

Treetop Star

Pin the inner star to the background fabric just above the top of the Christmas tree, then pin the 5 outer star points between the points of the inner star. Appliqué in place.

Feathered Stars

1. Cut 1" (2.5 cm) wide red and green fabric strips. Sew together 3 strips, alternating colors. Press. Cut the end of a sewn strip at a 45° angle. Make subsequent cuts, 1³/₈" (3.5 cm) from the first cut. Make 52 and 52r diamond sets. Reserve the remaining strips for Step 2.

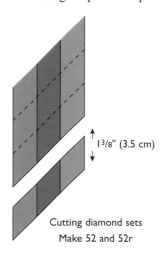

1³/₈" (3.5 cm)

Cutting diamond sets
Make 52 and 52r

2. Cut 1" (2.5 cm) wide strips from yellow fabric. Sew a yellow strip to 1 end of a pieced red and green strip. Cut diamond strips as above. Make 52 and 52r diamond sets.

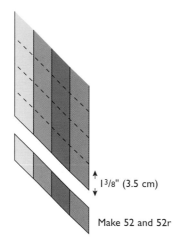

1³/₈" (3.5 cm)

Make 52 and 52r

3. Use 4 A and Ar setting units, 4 corner squares, and 4 side triangles to create the Feathered Star blocks as shown. Make 13 blocks.

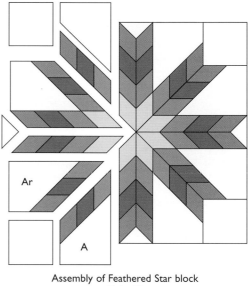

Assembly of Feathered Star block
Make 13

4. Sew a row of 5 Feathered Star blocks to the bottom of the quilt top. Press.

5. Sew a row of 8 Feathered Star blocks to the left side of the quilt top. Press.

Holly Berries and Vine

1. Measure the quilt top vertically through the center. Cut the right side inner border to this length and sew to the quilt top. Press seam toward the border.

2. Appliqué the holly vine border, holly leaves, and holly berries to right side and top of the quilt.

Borders

1. Measure the quilt top vertically through the center. Cut the outer side borders to this length and sew to the quilt top. Press seams toward the borders.

2. Measure the quilt top horizontally through the center. Cut the outer top and bottom borders to this length and sew to the quilt top. Press the seams toward the outer borders.

Snowfall

Scatter miniature snowballs in random sizes in the upper half of the quilt and extending some of them down the outer borders. Appliqué in place and then press.

Finishing

1. Layer and baste the quilt top, batting, and backing.

2. Quilt an assortment of linear and curved shapes in the center field of the quilt. Quilt cables in various widths in the borders.

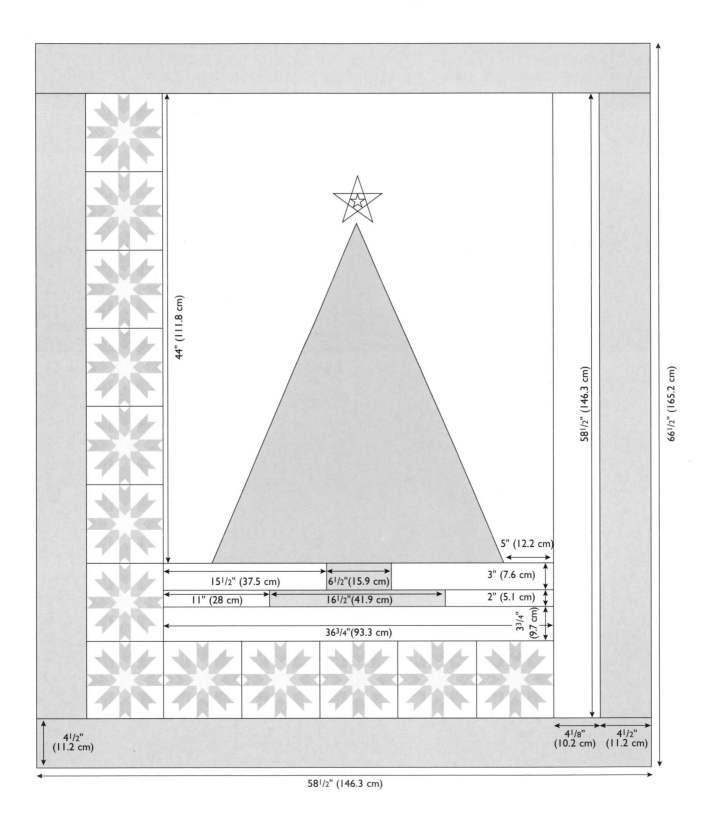

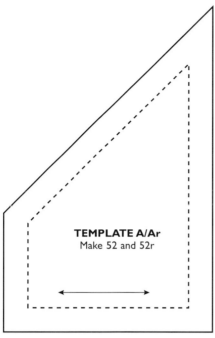

TEMPLATE A/Ar
Make 52 and 52r

Star setting unit

TEMPLATE D
Make 60

Holly leaf
Add turn-under allowance

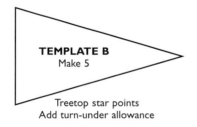

TEMPLATE B
Make 5

Treetop star points
Add turn-under allowance

TEMPLATE C
Make I

Treetop star center
Add turn-under allowance

Make 60

TEMPLATE E
Holly berry
Add turn-under allowance

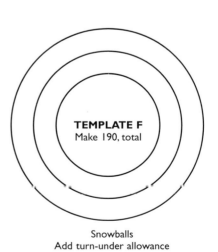

TEMPLATE F
Make 190, total

Snowballs
Add turn-under allowance

Silver Trees Projects

Silver Trees Quilt

MADE BY: Fumiko Shimizu
PHOTO BY: Masaki Yamamoto

FINISHED SIZE: 67¼" × 86" (170.8 cm × 218.4 cm)
FINISHED BLOCK SIZE: 4⅞" × 4¾" (12.1 cm × 12.4 cm)
TECHNIQUES: Piecing/Appliqué

This winter quilt has been a long-time favorite among C&T's Quilts Japan *fans. One reason for its appeal is the unique pewter/silver and white color palette with the rosy accents and another is the clever hand quilting that finishes the quilt.* Silver Trees *is both simple and elegant. For easier piecing, a simplified star appliqué replaces the pieced stars in the photo.*

FABRIC REQUIREMENTS

U.S.		METRIC
6¾ yards	Pale gray for tree blocks, borders, and binding	6 meters
6 yards, total	Assorted light and medium prints, tones-on-tone, and solids in gray, beige, cream, and pink for trees, mountains, and stars	5.5 meters, total
72" × 90"	Batting	180 cm × 225 cm
5 yards	Backing	4.5 meters

CUTTING

U.S.	PALE GRAY	METRIC
1½" × 3¼"	Tree background E: Cut 216.	3.7 cm × 8.2 cm
1½" × 2⅝"	Tree background F: Cut 216.	3.7 cm × 6.7 cm
1½" × 2¼"	Tree background G: Cut 432.	3.7 cm × 5.7 cm
1⅜" × 2½"	Tree background H: Cut 216.	3.4 cm × 6.3 cm
1½" × 5⅜"	Vertical sashing: Cut 96.	3.7 cm × 13.4 cm
1½" × 51¼"	Horizontal sashing: Cut 11.	3.7 cm × 129.2 cm
8½" × 70"	Side borders: Cut 2.	21.2 cm × 175.1 cm
8½" × 67¼"	Top and bottom borders: Cut 2.	21.2 cm × 169.2 cm
2¼" × 320"	Binding: Cut on straight of grain and double folded.	5.7 cm × 810 cm

U.S.	FABRICS IN GRAY, BEIGE, CREAM, AND PINK	METRIC
1½" × 3¼"	Treetop A: Cut 108.	3.7 cm × 8.3 cm
1½" × 4½"	Tree branch B: Cut 108.	3.7 cm × 11.5 cm
1½" × 5¼"	Tree branch C: Cut 216.	3.7 cm × 13.4 cm
1⅜" × 1¼"	Tree trunk D: Cut 108.	3.4 cm × 3.1 cm
Template A	Mountains: Cut 50, adjust template to vary sizes.	Template A
Template B	4-Pointed star: Cut 21.	Template B

Note: 2 trees can be made from a 1½" (3.8 cm) strip cut across the width of fabric.
Cut 54 strips to make 108 trees.

Construction of Christmas Tree Blocks

Note: Each block needs tree pieces A, B, C, D, and tree backgrounds E, F, G, and H.

1. Match the corner of a Background E to the corner of Treetop A, right sides together. Sew a diagonal seam. Trim $1/4$" (0.6 cm) from the sewn line and then press toward the treetop.

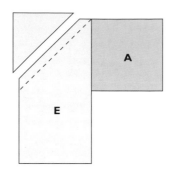

Match corners and sew E to A
Trim $1/4$" (0.6 cm) from sewn line

2. Repeat for the other side of the treetop. Make 108 treetop rows.

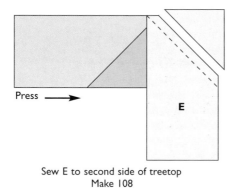

Sew E to second side of treetop
Make 108

3. Repeat the steps to make the additional tree branch rows. Sew a Background F to each side of Tree Branch B. Sew a Background G to each side of Tree Branch C. Sew another Background G to each side of another Tree Branch C. Make 108 of each tree branch row. (Note that the second and third rows are identical.) Press toward the tree branches.

4. To make the tree trunk, sew a Background H piece to each side of the Tree Trunk D piece. Press seams toward the trunk. Make 108 tree trunk rows.

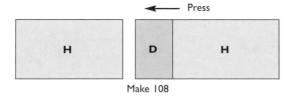

Make 108

5. Sew the 5 tree rows to make 1 tree block. Press. Trim the block to measure $5\,1/4$" wide x $5\,3/8$" high (13.2 cm x 13.4 cm). Make 108 blocks.

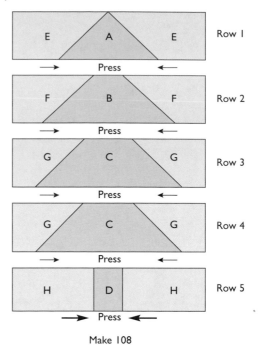

Make 108

Quilt Assembly

1. Sew 8 vertical sashing strips between 9 Christmas tree blocks. Press seams toward the sashing strips. Make 12 rows of Christmas tree blocks.

2. Measure the width of the Christmas tree block rows. Note the average width. This is the measurement for the horizontal sashing strips. Cut 11 sashing strips and then sew them in place between the Christmas tree block rows.

3. Appliqué mountains as desired to the side and bottom borders before attaching the borders to the quilt top. Reserve some mountains for the corners, but do not stitch them in place until after the borders are sewn to the quilt top. This will leave space for the mountains on the bottom border to overlap the mountains on the side borders and some of the Christmas tree blocks.

4. Use the star template to create the star and use the appliqué method of your choice to attach the stars to the horizontal sashing between the tree blocks.

Finishing

1. After all the borders have been stitched to the quilt top and the last mountains appliquéd to the corners, layer and baste the quilt top, batting, and backing.

2. Outline quilt around each Christmas tree and then quilt a diagonal grid in the background. Quilt a narrow cable design in the sashing strips. Quilt curved lines in the mountains and snowflakes and tiny snowballs in the remaining borders.

Finishing the appliqué

Quilt Assembly

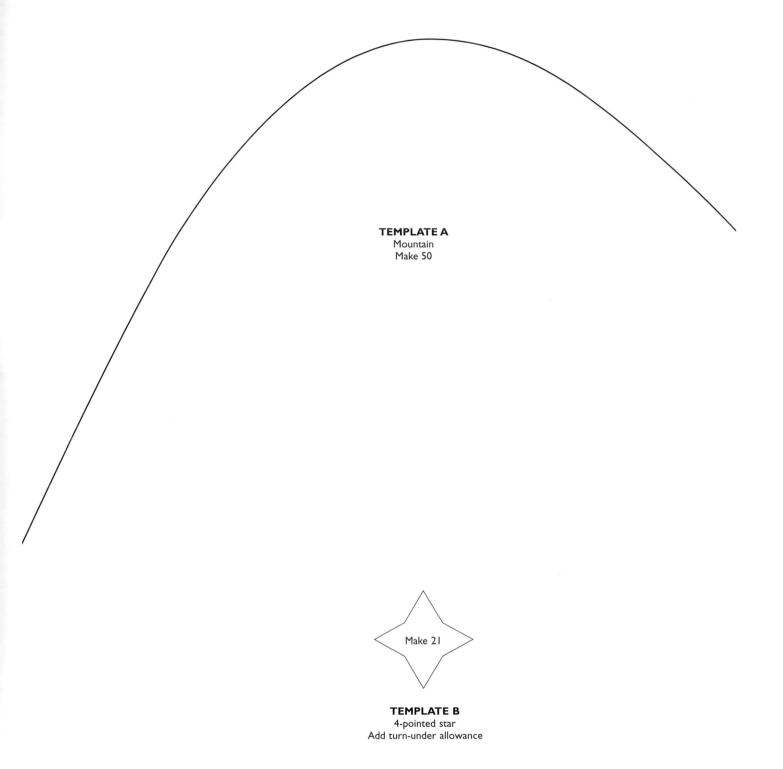

TEMPLATE A
Mountain
Make 50

Make 21

TEMPLATE B
4-pointed star
Add turn-under allowance

Silver Trees Pillow

MADE BY: Fumiko Shimizu
PHOTO BY: Masaki Yamamoto
FINISHED SIZE: 18 1/4" × 18 5/8" (46.4 cm × 47.3 cm)
FINISHED BLOCK SIZE: 4 3/4" × 4 7/8" (12 cm × 12.2 cm)
TECHNIQUES: Piecing/Appliqué

This pretty accent pillow adds just the right frosty touch to wintertime decor.

PROJECT REQUIREMENTS

U.S.		METRIC
1 1/2 yards	Silver or gray fabric for blocks, borders, and backing	1.2 meters
1/4 yard, total	Floral prints or tone-on-tone fabrics for Christmas tree blocks	25 cm
7" square	White for stars	20 cm square
20" × 20"	Batting	50 cm × 50 cm
5/8 yard	Lining	60 cm
15" × 15"	Pillow form	38 cm × 38 cm

CUTTING

U.S.	SILVER OR GRAY FABRIC	METRIC
5 1/4" × 5 3/8"	Plain blocks: Cut 4.	13.3 cm × 13.5 cm
1 1/2" × 3 1/4"	Tree background E: Cut 10.	3.7 cm × 8.2 cm
1 1/2" × 2 5/8"	Tree background F: Cut 10.	3.7 cm × 6.7 cm
1 1/2" × 2 1/4"	Tree background G: Cut 20.	3.7 cm × 5.7 cm
1 3/8" × 2 1/2"	Tree background H: Cut 10.	3.4 cm × 6.2 cm
2 1/2" × 15 1/8"	Side borders: Cut 2.	6.2 cm × 38.4 cm
2 1/2" × 18 3/4"	Top and bottom borders: Cut 2.	6.2 cm × 47.5 cm
20" × 20"	Backing: Cut 2.	50 cm × 50 cm

U.S.	SILVER OR GRAY FABRIC	METRIC
Template A	4-Pointed stars: Cut 6.	Template A

U.S.	FLORAL PRINTS OR TONE-ON-TONE FABRICS	METRIC
1¹/₂" x 3¹/₄"	Treetop A: Cut 5.	3.7 cm x 8.3 cm
1¹/₂" x 4¹/₂"	Tree branch B: Cut 5.	3.7 cm x 11.5 cm
1¹/₂" x 5¹/₄"	Tree branch C: Cut 10.	3.7 cm x 13.4 cm
1³/₈" x 1¹/₄"	Tree trunk D: Cut 5.	3.4 cm x 3.1 cm

Note: 2 trees can be made from a 1¹/₂" (3.8 cm) strip cut across the width of fabric. Cut 3 strips for the 5 trees.

Project Assembly

I. Refer to the Silver Trees Quilt project on page 58 for instructions on piecing the Christmas tree blocks. Make 5.

2. Appliqué 3 stars onto each of 2 background squares, making sure to leave ¹/₂" (1.2 cm) seam allowance around the perimeter.

Placement of 4-Pointed stars

3. Assemble the pillow top as shown. Press the seams toward the plain blocks.

4. Sew the side borders to the pillow top and press the seams toward the borders. Sew the top and bottom borders to the pillow top and press the seams toward the borders.

Finishing

I. Layer and baste the pillow top with the batting and lining.

2. Echo quilt around each Christmas tree. Scatter quilted snowflakes and tiny snowballs, but do not quilt the borders yet.

3. Hem 1 side of each backing piece. Overlap the hemmed pieces at least 8" (20 cm) and pin them to the pillow top, making sure the overlapped pieces are centered on the pillow top. Trim all edges even and square the corners.

Preparing pillow backing

4. Use a ¹/₄" (0.6 cm) seam allowance to sew all sides. Trim the corners and turn the pillow top to the right side. Push out the corners and press.

5. To create the flanged pillow edge, sew-in-the-ditch between the borders and blocks, about 1³/₄" (4.4 cm) from the outside edge. Quilt 2 more lines, ¹/₂" (1.2 cm) apart, between the first stitched line and the pillow edge as shown.

Pillow top assembly

6. Insert the pillow form into the pillow cover.

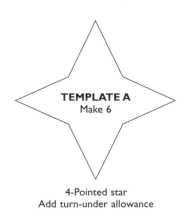

TEMPLATE A
Make 6

4-Pointed star
Add turn-under allowance

Index

About the Editors

Jennifer Rounds is a professional quiltmaker and a freelance writer. She writes the "Feature Teacher" column for *The Quilter* magazine. Her other titles with C&T Publishing include: *A Bouquet of Quilts* and *Wine Country Quilts* (with Cyndy Lyle Rymer) and *A Floral Affair* (with Catherine Comyns). Jennifer lives in Walnut Creek, California.

Catherine Comyns is a retired Registered Nurse who has made a second career out of her lifelong passion for quiltmaking. Besides making award-winning quilts, she promotes the art and craft of quiltmaking in her work as a teacher, designer, and judge. *Winter Wonders* is her second book. Catherine lives in Pleasant Hill, California.

Other Fine Books From C&T Publishing

For more information, ask for a free catalog:
C&T Publishing, Inc.
P.O. Box 1456
Lafayette, CA 94549
(800) 284-1114
Email: ctinfo@ctpub.com
Website: www.ctpub.com

For quilting supplies:
Cotton Patch Mail Order
3405 Hall Lane, Dept.CTB
Lafayette, CA 94549
(800) 835-4418
(925) 283-7883
Email: quiltusa@yahoo.com
Website: www.quiltusa.com

Note: Fabrics used in the quilts shown may not be currently available
beause fabric manufacturers keep most fabrics in print for only a
short time.